Praise for
Magnetic

"This book should be read by every single Christian teenage girl (even girls past teen years who are single). It is brilliant in concept, full of scripture, easy to read, impactful, and will keep the short attention span of busy teens and college girls. I give my friend Lynn and this book my highest endorsement!"

— LYSA TERKEURST, *New York Times* best-selling
author of *Unglued* and *Made to Crave,* and president
of Proverbs 31 Ministries

"*Magnetic* makes an ideal study for young women who are eager to get their focus on who they really are and what matters most in life. Lynn's conversational style draws you in from the first chapter, and by the end you feel as if you've made a new friend. Be prepared to be challenged and changed as you read this lovely book."

— ROBIN JONES GUNN, best-selling author of the Christy
Miller series, *Praying For Your Future Husband,* and
*Spoken For: Embracing Who You Are and Whose
You Are*

"The message of this book is exactly what I want my teenage daughter to hear: 'You have a deep desire to be loved and admired, but focus on finding the love of Jesus first. Focus on developing and living out the fruits of the Spirit. And that is what will cause you to shine before a watching world.' Thank you, Lynn, for this personal message that every teenage girl will find magnetic."

— SHAUNTI FELDHAHN, social researcher and best-selling
author of *For Women Only* and *For Young Women Only*

"In a culture where teen girls are bombarded with false messages about what makes them attractive to boys, *Magnetic* offers a different and Jesus-honoring way. Lynn's engaging 'I've been there' style will draw teens in as they encounter a mentor's heart passionately poured out on the pages. Full of biblical truths tucked strategically inside relevant stories, and laced throughout with practical 'apply it now' tools, this book should be in the backpack of every teen girl you know!"

  —KAREN EHMAN, Proverbs 31 Ministries speaker
   and author of seven books including *LET. IT. GO.*
   and *Everyday Confetti*

"With the heart of a friend who gets you and a mentor who loves you, Lynn Cowell will help you (the girl God loves) become all He created you to be! In the powerful message of *Magnetic,* you will discover the balance between wanting the attention of a guy and embracing the unconditional love of the most important Guy! Learn how to laugh more and worry less about what others think, while developing irresistible beauty and investing in relationships that bring out the best version of the girl God created you to be!"

  —RENEE SWOPE, best-selling author of *A Confident*
   Heart and Proverbs 31 Ministries radio co-host
   for *Everyday Life with Lysa & Renee*

"Every girl wants to be magnetic. Every girl needs to read this book. You'll find it entertaining and full of endearing advice. Lynn Cowell has provided the total package in this book once again!"

  —BEKAH HAMRICK MARTIN, author of *The Bare Naked Truth*

"My friend Lynn Cowell really knows how to tap into teen girls' hearts. Her book *Magnetic* is relatable, memorable, and breaks the mold of typical teen books. This book will be on the must-read list for my three daughters!"

—Nicki Koziarz, writer, speaker, and Proverbs 31 Ministries online Bible study coordinator

"Lynn has a God-given ability to reach the depths of a teen girl's heart with the message of love Jesus has for her. Magnetic is an invitation for teen girls to trade boyfriend-based identities for a forever *agape* identity in Jesus Christ."

—Erin Bishop, founder and president of the Whatever Girls Ministry

"Every girl needs a mentor who points her to true north and helps her navigate the challenges of life. Lynn Cowell is that mentor. In a world that offers so many confusing messages for young girls, Lynn gives clear direction and profound wisdom along the journey. This is the book every teen girl needs to read!"

—Jill Savage, CEO of Hearts at Home and author of *No More Perfect Moms*

"In *Magnetic,* Lynn Cowell has done an amazing job of guiding the reader in how to put godly desires into action. Lynn challenges readers with these words: 'Your choices today shape the woman you'll be tomorrow. Who do you want to be?' I believe this book will help young women understand how the fruits of the Spirit make them magnetic, shining in their hearts and showing through their actions."

—Sharie King, wife of Clayton King and author of *True Love Project* and *12 Questions to Ask Before You Marry*

Magnetic

Magnetic

Becoming the Girl He Wants

Lynn Cowell

MULTNOMAH

Magnetic

Details in some anecdotes and stories have been changed to protect the identities of the persons involved.

Trade Paperback ISBN 978-1-60142-580-5
eBook ISBN 978-1-60142-581-2

Cover design by Mark D. Ford

Published in association with the literary agency of the Fedd Agency Inc., P.O. Box 341973, Austin, TX 78734.

Published in the United States by Multnomah, an imprint of the Crown Publishing Group, a division of Penguin Random House LLC, New York.

MULTNOMAH® and its mountain colophon are registered trademarks of Penguin Random House LLC.

Library of Congress Cataloging-in-Publication Data
Cowell, Lynn, 1967–
    Magnetic : becoming the girl he wants / Lynn Cowell. — First Edition.
        pages cm
    Includes bibliographical references.
    ISBN 978-1-60142-580-5 — ISBN 978-1-60142-581-2 (electronic) 1. Fruit of the Spirit.
2. Women—Conduct of life. I. Title.
    BV4501.3.C697 2014
    248.8'43—dc23

                                                    2014018122

Printed in the United States of America
2018

10 9 8 7 6 5

SPECIAL SALES
Most Multnomah books are available at special quantity discounts when purchased in bulk by corporations, organizations, and special-interest groups. Custom imprinting or excerpting can also be done to fit special needs. For information, please e-mail specialmarketscms@penguin randomhouse.com or call 1-800-603-7051.

To my mom, Lila Martin Parker,
and
my mom-in-love, Annette Cowell.

Thank you for showing me through your daily walks with Jesus
what it truly means to be magnetic.

Contents

Acknowledgments

Jesus, thank You for all You've done for me, none of which I could come close to deserving. Your goodness to me never ceases to amaze me. I am so very, very thankful for the love You pour into my heart each and every day. You've given rich meaning to my life!

Greg, I was one blessed girl the day you decided I was the girl you wanted! From the first day we started dating, you have supported and cheered for me every step of the way. I could never do what God has called me to do without you, but more important, I wouldn't want to. I love you!

Zach, Mariah, and Madi—I so appreciate you listening to my ideas, reading my writings, and encouraging me every step of the way while I was writing this book. I pray the Lord will be gracious to you as you become the man and women He created you to be! You're my treasure and I love you so!

My families, Martin and Cowell—how blessed I am to have *all* my family members love Jesus! You're the best!

Lysa, Renee, Glynnis, and Samantha, how grateful I am for your continual investment in my life! You all have pushed me to be a better writer, a more powerful speaker, and most of all, a woman who follows after God with all my heart. Thank you for living it out so I can follow!

Esther, thank you for believing in this message. Because you use the gifts God has given you for Him, the doors were opened for me to use mine. I am so very grateful!

Renee, thank you for using your gifts to help me make *Magnetic* the best it could be!

My sisters and friends at Proverbs 31 Ministries, what an honor to invest in the lives of women of all ages with you. I am grateful for such an honor!

Laura, my editor at WaterBrook Multnomah—thank you for taking my thoughts and words and massaging them with your beautiful touch. Thank you, friend!

Bonnie, Julie, Kathy, Kelly, and Loretta—my prayer-filled friends. A girl is blessed when she has one amazingly loyal friend. How God gave me five, I'll never know! Thank you for your constant words of encouragement and prayers. You're the best!

Thank you, Alexandra, Anne, Annie, Dianna, Lindsey, and Madi for sharing your time and hearts with me. You girls are so precious to me! I love you!

To all the guys who shared their stories and opinions for *Magnetic,* I couldn't have written this story without your words. Thank you for helping me to invest in girls!

And to my readers, both girls and their moms—thank you for your hearts to become the women He wants you to be! I know Jesus is saying, "Well done!"

The Power to Become Magnetic

The Captivating Characteristics That Make a Girl Gorgeous

Why doesn't he like me? I just couldn't figure it out. *What is it about me that isn't as attractive as her? Am I not as pretty? Am I too loud? Are my friends not cool enough?* The questions gnawed at me, eating away at my confidence. He had liked me once; surely I could get him to like me again. There had to be a way.

I was determined to find out what was wrong with me.

Maybe it was my body. Once, when I was surrounded by people who already intimidated me, my "friend" Dave called out, "Hey, Lynn, why do you bother wearing a bra? You're so flat, you should just wear Band-Aids." If only I could have evaporated into thin air.

Then again, maybe it was my hair. Not only was it curly, it was out of control. Dave nicknamed me Lucy, as in Lucy from the cartoon *Peanuts*. Not exactly the image you'd find under *hot* on Wikipedia. I wondered if her hair was the reason Schroeder, the piano dude, never asked her out.

Flat and frizzy…I convinced myself these were the reasons I couldn't attract Greg, the guy I wanted. Maybe I never would. It seemed I didn't have what it took to get this guy.

Do you ever wonder…

What does she have that I haven't got?

Why doesn't he ask me out?

What makes her so popular? Why not me?

What's wrong with me?

Do you sometimes feel as if your life's equation is Boy + Me = Valuable?

Invisible to Perfect Guy, it's easy to think, *The problem must be imperfect me.* Maybe you've even tried fixing "the problem":

Hair: new color, new cut. *Check.*

Clothes: cute outfit. *Check.*

Friends: do what it takes to become more popular. *Working on it.*

Body: join the gym. *Ask Mom and Dad.*

Yet, no matter how hard you try, it's never enough.

THE MAGNETIC ATTRACTION

Back in my own "wish I were dating" days, my highs and lows depended on whether or not I saw *him* in the hall; my happiness was determined by whether or not *he* noticed me. The crush I had was crushing me.

I wish there had been someone who could have helped me. Although maybe I wouldn't have listened. But I wish someone could have shown me that the longing in my heart pointed not to my need for a guy, but to my deeper need for something even greater. That I was created to be loved perfectly and unconditionally, made to have my heart filled each and every day with love from the Perfect Man, Jesus.

I wish someone could have shown me I am valuable just as I am, created for an amazing purpose—and nothing on this planet should hold me back from my purpose, especially not some guy!

Then I could have spent my time, energy, and emotions, not on a guy I didn't have, but on the One I did. I could have moved from obsessing over why I wasn't wanted to becoming the type of girl a guy would want. Not just as someone to date but as the one he'd want to spend the rest of his life with.

Nothing on this planet should hold you back from your purpose, especially not some guy!

I remember making the list, a gargantuan description of everything I was looking for in the guy I would marry one day. The more powerful list would have described the woman I wanted to become, the woman he couldn't resist!

What would happen if you made the switch now? Shifted your focus off a guy and onto the Guy?

What if, together, we discovered an irresistible beauty deeper than designer clothes, skinny jeans, and flawless skin? A confidence so attractive, nothing could cause us to lose it? A glamour simply magnetic?

In my quest to discover true beauty, I began to see *gorgeous* as much more than the face in my mirror. *Gorgeous* is not skin deep but heart deep, a beauty that develops as my heart discovers and returns true love.

This beauty, this attractiveness, is found in the girl who has what I call captivating characteristics—what the Bible calls the fruit of the Spirit. These heart traits are described in Galatians 5:22–23: love, joy, peace, patience, kindness, goodness, faithfulness, gentleness, and self-control.

Let's unpack what the Bible means by the fruit of the Spirit. Picture a gorgeous piece of fruit, a luscious and juicy Florida orange. The bright and plump skin calls, "Peel me!" As you pull back the skin, juice squirts everywhere. This orange is just the kind Tropicana looks for!

Then there is another orange. Puny and shriveled. Something on the tree went terribly wrong. Bugs, disease, lack of sun? Whatever the reason, the orange never reached its full potential. Dried up, the ugly fruit is no use to anyone!

What caused the drastic difference between these two pieces of fruit? One so beautiful, the other so…not? The juicy orange, pleasingly healthy, drew in all it needed to reach its full potential. Sunshine, water, and nutrients from the soil nurtured the fruit into the fullness it was created for. The other orange did not absorb the nourishment it needed.

But the fruit of the Spirit is love, joy, peace, patience, kindness, goodness, faithfulness, gentleness, self-control; against such things there is no law.

Galatians 5:22-23, ESV

When you're planted in God, you become like the tangy, appealing fruit! He provides you with all you need to reach your full potential—to be the best *you* you can be!

That is one beautiful you!

Instead of chasing after the guy running from you, you're pursuing the One coming after you. In the process of seeking His heart, you'll become the amazing individual He designed you to be, a girl who is irresistibly magnetic, beautiful inside and out!

Think of the two pieces of fruit. Which one attracts your interest?

The same is true for guys. They are drawn to you when you are at your best, your greatest potential! So the *you* you become impacts who you'll attract. If that guy you're crushing on is mature and solid in his faith, he'll be attracted to a girl who is mature and solid in her faith. Notice I didn't say that the guy you're crushing on is going to return the favor. I am saying that the type of guy who will be drawn to you is someone who shares your priorities and passions. A guy who is like you is the guy who will like you.

You're thinking, *Yeah right! I don't see this happening. You obviously haven't been to my school. You have no clue what guys are like; there aren't any of that type of guys, the godly guys, out there.*

I agree there aren't too many guys pursuing God. But check this out: there aren't too many girls pursuing God either! The few guys I have met who are running hard after Jesus, though, are keeping their eyes open for a girl who is doing the same.

GORGEOUS GLORIFIES GOD

Have you ever met a girl who has a genuine love for other people? Instead of being focused on herself, she focuses on others, making those around her feel wanted, special, valued. There is something so beautiful about her!

Think of a girl you know who's joyful. She looks on the bright side. You feel good just being around her! Who doesn't want to be close to a girl like that? She's more fun to hang out with than the one constantly complaining.

What about the one resisting the pull of girl drama, refusing to get dragged into arguments or backbiting? She's peaceful, her calm outlook refreshing.

Got a friend who never uses the word *annoyed*? Patient with others, her time is your time. Every conversation doesn't have to be about her; she really listens and cares.

Think of a girl you'd describe as kind and good. Every person is important and valuable to her. She never says "I was only joking," because she doesn't have a rude comment to cover up.

Have a friend you can tell anything? Your secret's placed in a vault when you tell her. You have no fear of your secret slipping out; she's faithful. She'll be your friend through everything.

How about the girl who is gentle, not controlled by peer pressure, not obnoxious or attention seeking? Comfortable with who she is, she's intentional about her choices because her priority is honoring herself and her God.

A girl like that is magnetic. Who could resist wanting to be around her?

Guess what? You can be that girl!

How?

These magnetic traits are the result, or fruit, of the girl who has given her entire life to Jesus. She now spends her emotional energy allowing Him to live His life through her.

Now, you don't have to burn yourself out trying to become perfect. These gorgeous qualities will show up as you spend time with God and He pours His perspective into you!

GET UP AND GET GROWING

To help you toward your goal of becoming the girl He wants, we're going to investigate these captivating characteristics together.

Right now I'm picturing you joining me on a Thursday night when my living room is filled with a group of girls who love Jesus and are trying to figure life out. We've been getting together for about five years, learning more about God and ourselves. I know you'd fit right in!

If you don't have your own group, you can start one! Pull a group of your friends together, make a snack, and go through *Magnetic* together. Of course, it's also perfectly okay to do this with just the two of you: Jesus and you.

As you go along, you'll find questions to help you see how the fruit of the Spirit can grow in your life. You'll also find lots of insights from girls much like you as well as comments from godly guys about what they find attractive. I interviewed both guys who have found their own magnetic girl and those who are still looking. Their comments are really revealing!

I love quizzes, so I've included one for each of the captivating characteristics. In the back of the book, you'll find a chart where you can record your score for each one. This way you can identify which of the captivating characteristics are your strengths and which are areas where you need to grow. You'll find the chart on page 187. Try folding down the corner of that page to make it easy to find quickly.

As we're going through *Magnetic,* sometimes you might feel like change in your life is coming fast. Then a bad day will trip you up and you'll think, *I've not changed at all*. Not true! You are growing; you just had a setback. Get up and get going! Just keep on taking small steps, one after another, as Jesus leads you to become the girl He wants.

Grab your Bible and a journal, and let's do it! Let's learn what it means to be magnetic!

It's (Not) All About Me

Love Compels Confident Consideration of Others

Give up a Friday night? No way! The way Kalley saw it, the sweet-sixteen party invitation from Allie meant one thing: boredom! Even if Allie was one of her best friends, Kalley wasn't going to spend a Friday night hanging out with people she didn't like. *After being in school all week, I deserve to do what I want,* she told herself. *It's my weekend, right?*

So why did she feel sick when the invitation hit the bottom of the trash?

The choice: Do I choose to please me or please someone else?

I struggle with this constantly! My schizophrenic heart pushes one way, then pulls me the other. My thoughts toss me back and forth between *I could* and *I should.* Make time for my friend who needs a friend? Ignore the call because I'm feeling tired? Volunteer to help, even on my day off? I wrestle with my wants. Deep down, I know the right answer is tied to *would*. What would love do?

How about you and your choices? Help with the laundry or watch TV? Sit with old friends or welcome the new girl? Go to the movies or help at the homeless shelter? The best answer for all these questions and more is another question: *What would love do?*

How's Your Love Life?

Add up the points for each answer you select and compare your total to the love scale at the bottom.

A) The athletically challenged guy trips in gym. You...
   1. reenact the scene for your friends who missed it.
   2. laugh to yourself.
   3. don't draw attention to him.

B) A friend is spending the night when your crush texts. You...
   1. spend the evening texting him and reading his every word.
   2. check in every thirty minutes to keep things rolling.
   3. text him to say, "I'm with a friend. Available tomorrow?"

C) Your friends forget your birthday. You...
   1. purposefully "forget" theirs.

To answer that question, first we have to know what love is. You love stylish boots, and you love your dog. You love your parents, and you love your boyfriend. Obviously, not all love is the same!

Love that is a fruit of the Spirit means "to cherish, esteem, or respect; to be concerned about, devoted to, and loyal." How often would you say your choices are guided by *this* kind of love?

---

    2. express your feelings clearly on social media.

    3. believe they wouldn't hurt your feelings on purpose.

D) You find out a classmate is pregnant. You...

    1. say, "I knew she was that kind."

    2. whisper the news to another girl.

    3. pray she has the strength to carry her baby.

How did you do? If you got...

    10–12 points: Beautifully magnetic! You love others more than yourself.

    7–9 points: Sometimes you put others first, but your "love life" needs some attention.

    4–6 points: Ready to gain a better understanding of love?

Be sure to record your score in the back of the book, so you can identify your strengths as well as the areas where you need to seek God's help.

THE HEART AND SOUL OF LOVE

The girl who chooses others above herself is rare. She's hard to find but easy to spot. Showing love with her actions, not just a bunch of words, makes her stand out and causes others to want to be around her.

Adam's story reveals how attractive a girl becomes when she's all about giving love instead of getting love. "I was first attracted to Lindsay because of her smile and eyes. What attracted me the most," he continued, "was how Lindsay wanted to listen when I talked; she was engaged in our conversation. Those conversations were meaningful; she wanted more in life. I was drawn to the heart and soul behind the smile and eyes. Because Lindsay isn't wrapped up in talking about herself all the time, she pulls out of me what no one else can."

Since Adam sometimes led worship in church, he often felt girls were interested in him because of what he did rather than for who he was. But through her genuine interest in him—her choice to esteem and respect him—Lindsay showed Adam true love. True love is about seeking the best for another rather than getting something for ourselves. Adam recognized a difference between Lindsay's behavior and the interest he'd previously gotten from girls, whose primary concern was drawing attention to themselves.

So where did Lindsay learn this unselfish sort of love—and how can we get it too?

It begins with the love the Father has for us. He demonstrated unconditional love when He sent His Son, Jesus. He didn't just say He loved us; His actions also showed He cherished us and was concerned for our well-being. Even though we deserved to pay for our sins by being eternally separated from Him, God instead demonstrated unconditional love by sending His perfect Son, Jesus, to pay the price for our sins. He chose what was best for us, clearing the way for us to be together forever with Him. First John 3:16 tells it this way: "This is how we know what love is: Jesus Christ laid down his life for us."

TRUE LOVE LAYS ASIDE SELFISHNESS

Have you ever thought, *I sure would look good next to that guy!* I have! My husband stands six foot two and has dark wavy hair. Need I say more? But if it's all about how that gorgeous guy makes us look or feel, then ours is only selfish love.

Selfish love? Those two words seem like opposites. Can selfish love even exist?

Even though we know the word *love* can include lots of different emotions and feelings, the English language doesn't give us a lot of options when it comes to describing all that variety. But the New Testament part of the Bible was written in Greek, which offers several words for *love*. Understanding these different types of love can help us figure out whether it's even possible to experience selfish love.

Eros love is the one we see most often in the movies. Maybe your friend told you, "I'm in love! Every time I get around him, it's like nothing I've ever felt before!" Your friend's probably feeling *erao,* or *eros,* the Greek word for intense or passionate love. Much of the emotion associ-

When I make love all about **me**, I ruin the chance to focus on **we**.

ated with this love is based on sexual feelings. These feelings are powerful! You can often spot *erao* because it's me centered, focused on how that person makes me feel and what I can do to feel that passion again. *Erao* can be thrilling—but when the excitement fades, so does this kind of love. When I make love all about *me,* I ruin the chance to focus on *we*.

Storgeo love occurs naturally. Think family, how you feel about your mom and dad, your grandparents, and maybe even your little brother—when he's asleep.

Phileo is friendship love. You feel love for your best friend because you like her; she's creative, funny, a blast to be around! She gets you. You like how you feel when you're with her.

Agape, the Greek word for the kind of love we read about in the fruit-of-the-Spirit list, stands apart from all other kinds of love. *Agape* is not shallow; it's not wrapped up in my physical or emotional feelings. *Agape* is not all about me; it's concerned about what's best for the *other* person. Even if it's not returned, *agape keeps giving,* which makes it powerfully attractive and unique. In *agape,* I deliberately make a decision to love another person, to value him not because of anything that person has done or can do for me but simply because that person is precious. I choose to prize him, to be devoted to, appreciate, and respect that human.

Have you ever experienced *agape* love? When?

. . . .
. . . .
. . . .
. . . .

Agape is the true love God modeled when He sent His Son, making up His mind to choose us, to put our need for love and forgiveness first. Love is the core of who Jesus is. Since we are His, love should be who we are too! For example, if Kalley's goal is to become magnetic, she needs to decide what action shows *agape* love to Allie: going to the party or going her own way. Her decision shows whether or not she truly appreciates her friend. With the power of the Holy Spirit, she can choose unselfish love.

With Jesus's love, there are no strings attached, no hidden motives, no keeping score. And understanding His love helps us become the girl He wants us to become. Before we can love someone else, we need to be filled by His perfect love. When we understand it, we can show it. Consider Paul's prayer in Ephesians:

> And I pray that you, being rooted and established in love, may have power, together with all the saints, to grasp how wide and long and high and deep is the love of Christ, and to know this love that surpasses knowledge—that you may be filled to the measure of all the fullness of God. (Ephesians 3:17–19)

A LOVE THAT NEVER LETS GO

When we are filled with God's perfect love, we can't help but love others the same way.

If we don't first let His love fill and satisfy us, though, we'll keep looking to others to fill our empty hearts. We'll take risks in the hope of getting love and hanging on to it—hoping this time we've found someone who will always love us, never leave us, never reject us. We gamble our hearts, and we usually lose.

As a magnetic girl, you don't have to wait for a guy to fill your need for love and you don't have to live in fear of rejection. God's deep love ejects fear, bringing you supernatural confidence—confidence based not on your brains, your looks, your achievements, or your ability to attract a guy. Your confidence is

> There is no fear in love. But perfect love drives out fear, because fear has to do with punishment. The one who fears is not made perfect in love.
>
> **1 John 4:18**

built on His love, which never lets you go. Which means you can leave insecurity behind. There's no need to draw attention to yourself; in fact, you shift your attentions to others!

Here's a great verse every girl should have within reach. I memorized it so I'd have it whenever I need it! Put this one on your phone, in your agenda, or on your mirror. Let it soak deep into your heart:

> No, in all these things we are more than conquerors through
> him who loved us. For I am convinced that neither death nor
> life, neither angels nor demons, neither the present nor the
> future, nor any powers, neither height nor depth, nor anything
> else in all creation, will be able to separate us from the love of
> God that is in Christ Jesus our Lord. (Romans 8:37–39)

None of the things Paul listed can pull us away or come between us and God's perfect love for us. Not anything happening in our lives today or anything that will happen in the future has enough power to separate you and me from the love of God. What a confidence builder!

Ever seen a girl soon after she gets a new boyfriend? A permanent smile's on her face.

But what happens when the boy moves on? So does her confidence.

Not so with Jesus; He never moves on! He will always and forever be wild about you!

Lindsay totally gets this. She knows Jesus adores her, and since that's where her confidence is, she has been able to love Adam without fear of rejection. God's perfect love inside of her erases fear.

If you struggle with fear of others' rejection, there's still room for more of God's love in your heart! Fill up with the truth of how much He adores you! Then with the confidence of God's love, you, like Lindsay, can fearlessly take the risk of loving others. When His love naturally oozes out of your heart, you become simply irresistible! Others are naturally attracted to love.

THE LOVE CYCLE

As you get love from God, you can give love back to God and pass love on to others. It's what I call the love cycle. Jesus explains it in Matthew 22:37–39: "'Love the Lord your God with all your heart and with all your soul and with all your mind.' This is the first and greatest commandment. And the second is like it: 'Love your neighbor as yourself.'"

Lindsay understood the love of God. It filled her heart, allowing her to follow God's first command. And her love for God spilled over into love for others, including Adam. Lindsay chose to love Adam, not to see what she could get out of the relationship for herself but simply because she had love to share. Overflowing love cycled from God to Lindsay and then from Lindsay to God and to Adam. And this godly guy was irresistibly drawn to the fruit of the Spirit he saw blossoming in Lindsay. "Without love, none of the other fruits of the Spirit exist in the same way," he told me.

This all might feel a little strange to you if you've only experienced conditional love, the kind that waits for the other person to act first or that gives in order to get. To love without any expectation of return may sound like a good way to get your heart crushed. Won't constantly pouring out love on others leave you empty? Nope. Not if you're continually going to God as your source of love. God's love never runs out, so it can flow through us in a never-ending supply. "And so we know and rely on the love God has for us. God is love. Whoever lives in love lives in God, and God in him" (1 John 4:16).

Wear Love

For the girl who wants to be lovely, gorgeous, and stunning, the Bible tells us exactly what to wear. Check out Colossians 3:12–14:

> Therefore, as God's chosen people, holy and dearly loved, clothe yourselves with compassion, kindness, humility, gentleness and patience. Bear with each other and forgive whatever grievances you may have against one another. Forgive as the Lord forgave you. And over all these virtues put on love, which binds them all together in perfect unity.

When I am packing for a trip, I take my time! I've only got one shot to pack, so I want to select the perfect outfits. Shouldn't we take that same care when choosing how to dress our hearts? Paul says the perfect outfit is a combination of compassion, kindness, humility, gentleness, patience, and most important, love!

What is your favorite item in your closet? A pair of shoes? A comfy sweatshirt? A beautiful skirt? Jesus can work in us so love becomes what we feel most comfortable and beautiful in! Love fits every occasion. Like a new pair of shoes, at first living out God's love can feel uncomfortable, even unnatural in our me-first culture. As we are maturing, though, we'll grow more and more comfortable loving others, putting their needs and wants before our own.

Agape will rush out of us and spill over onto siblings, parents, friends, and even the barista and others we encounter throughout the day. And while such love will be appealing to a guy who shares your love for God, this isn't just about becoming attractive. For those of us who call ourselves Christ's, He commands us to love like He loves: unconditionally, no strings attached. "And he has given us this command: Whoever loves God must also love his brother" (1 John 4:21).

My daughter Madi listened to God's command when she faced a choice in her social calendar: go to the lake or serve the poor? Though she wanted more than anything to go to the lake with her friends, she made the difficult decision to serve the poor. She knew that's what love would do. Serving with friends from church for twenty-four continuous hours, they played kickball with homeless children, served lunch, cleaned a shelter, and created a BBQ party in a poor section of our city. Dirty feet never looked so good as when she sauntered up our steps afterward. Though she was worn out, I had never before seen her glow as she did that morning, with love pouring out of her. "That was so amazing," she said, as her backpack slid to the floor. "I've got to get to sleep, but first let me tell you about the past twenty-four hours."

As Madi told me all about her adventure with the poor and broken of our city, her bright eyes twinkled and her laugh was so pure. Loving others had created a beauty that could never come from designer clothes or makeup.

When did you recently choose loving others over loving yourself?

. . . .
. . . .
. . . .
. . . .

Selflessly loving others can be your beauty secret too! God's Word gives us clarity with everyday examples of what love looks like.

It looks like Jesus.

THE LOOK OF LOVE

First John 3:16 gives us a clear example of Christ's love: "This is how we know what love is: Jesus Christ laid down his life for us. And we ought to lay down our lives for our brothers." Jesus modeled laying down His life for us. He showed love by giving His life for our need. "If anyone has material possessions and sees his brother in need but has no pity on him, how can the love of God be in him?" (verse 17).

Generosity is an outward expression of love. When Mariah got a job as a nanny, she also got her first taste of being generous: "I really love the opportunity I have now to be able to bless someone. They are so surprised when I pay for their food or movie tickets." Of course you can be generous with more than just money—sharing your time, effort, knowledge, or talents.

Where will you show generosity in the next couple of days?

. . . .

. . . .

. . . .

. . . .

. . . .

Mariah understands that love is an action and a command to us from God. "Dear children, let us not love with words or tongue but with actions and in truth" (verse 18). It is so easy to tell our friends "Love ya!" or "I'm here for you!" but actually putting their best interests before our own is anything but!

God's Word makes clear what love is and what it is not. For now, let's highlight a few points on what love is not. If you want to dig further, check out 1 Corinthians 13. It's known as the love chapter.

Love Is Not Hateful

I know you have met the girl who seems all nice when you first meet her, but the moment things don't go her way, all kinds of ugly comes out. Let's admit it: we've all been that girl. Birthday plans tank. Someone subtweets about us. He breaks up. Ugly comes out.

But love never hates, not under any circumstances. It just isn't possible. "If anyone says, 'I love God,' yet hates his brother, he is a liar. For anyone who does not love his brother, whom he has seen, cannot love God, whom he has not seen" (1 John 4:20).

Love Is Not Envious

What girl hasn't struggled with envy? It snakes its way into our minds and then slithers down into our hearts. It may be envy about guys when we're younger, but when not brought under control, envy just moves on to something else as we get older. Her house, her shoes, her job. There's no such thing as a little bit of envy; it comes in and takes over. Impossible to hide, it's definitely ugly! For the magnetic girl, envy is never an option because 1 Corinthians 13:4 tells us that love "does not envy." When we sense envy creeping in, we have to be brutal, leaving no room for just a little bit. Otherwise, we're just setting ourselves up for misery. "A heart at peace gives life to the body, but envy rots the bones" (Proverbs 14:30).

What most often invites envy into your heart?

. . . .
. . . .
. . . .
. . . .
. . . .
. . . .

Love Is Not Rude

Rudeness has become so common in our culture, a symptom of our me-first syndrome.

Who are you most often tempted to be rude to? It seems in our house, it's easiest to be rude to those you know will always love you—family. But it doesn't stop there. Teachers. Friends. Sometimes we're even rude to those serving us.

What is going on in your heart and mind when you choose to be rude? Afraid to look dumb? Pouting because you didn't get your way? I've never seen a girl be rude after landing the lead part in the musical, but watch out if she didn't! She comments to others, "She can't act, can't sing, and can't dance!" Not getting her way, she resorts to being rude—and nobody wants to be around that.

Contrast the quick-to-complain girl with the one who handles disappointment, even rudeness, with style. She says, "I'm happy for her; she deserved it." That's the girl who stands out.

Let's set up a challenge: let's bring manners back into style…starting now! In the next twenty-four hours someone will be rude to you. Determine now that you won't pay back rudeness but pay out love.

Love Is Not Self-Seeking

I love what Adam said about Lindsay: "What attracted me the most was how Lindsay wanted to listen when I talked. She isn't wrapped up in talking about herself all the time." How refreshing!

Lindsay knows life is not all about her. Her selflessness shines as she notices and pays attention to those around her. Love is not self-seeking.

Love Does Not Keep Score

"You did that last time…"

"Here we go again…"

"You always…"

Ever start a sentence this way? If you hear yourself saying one of these lines, you can be sure you're keeping score. Keeping score has been a personal struggle for me—not so much what others have done wrong against me, but the nice things I've done for others not repaid. Either way, it's not love.

Wonder if you're keeping score? Listen to yourself. Do you feel the need to tell the story of how she let you down or how much it hurt when he broke up? If you can't get beyond retelling it again and again, then God's got some work to do and it starts with you forgiving.

Keeping score is your Check Heart signal. Like the Check Oil light on your car's dashboard, it says you need repair. First Corinthians 13:5 tells us love "keeps no record of wrongs." You'll know you've beaten bitterness when you no longer need to repeat the story of how you were mistreated.

 What story have you found yourself telling over and over? Say a prayer, forgiving that person and asking God to please give you the feelings to match your obedience.

. . . .
. . . .
. . . .
. . . .
. . . .
. . . .

Love Takes No Joy in the Distress of Others

Few things are as hard to resist as sharing juicy gossip! "Have you heard what happened with her?" Especially when it is something bad, that ugly girl in us wants to tell the world!

Let's be honest. Those of us who are Christ followers tend to be the worst. "She deserved it." "What does she expect when she acts like that?" Somehow we feel justified in celebrating when those who don't live God's way get what we think they deserve.

When you hear news about another girl's problems, what's your first response? Does your heart break when you learn of her unwise decision, or are you secretly glad?

It's hard to admit we can be so ugly, but confessing our sin is a necessary step toward becoming the girl He wants. When we take an honest look inside and see the sin blocking His love, we can humble ourselves and ask Jesus to change us. As long as we pretend we have it together, we won't!

Another's failure never makes us look better.

Finding happiness in someone else's trouble reveals a hard heart. Another's failure never makes us look better. Beauty comes when we allow Jesus to break our hearts for others the way His heart breaks for them.

The Bible calls the change we need *repentance,* meaning "deep sorrow or regret for a past wrong." It's not enough to admit we were wrong; we only grow by asking Christ to forgive us and make a permanent change in us. With Jesus's power, we can lean on Him for the power to go in His direction.

Ask the Holy Spirit to make you aware of how you respond to another person's bad news. Pray for a heart tender to the hurts of others. He promises us in Ezekiel 36:26, "I will give you a new heart and put a new spirit in you; I will remove from you your heart of stone and give you a heart of flesh."

Love hopes a situation turns out for good, rather than hoping for the worst. Love sincerely wants the best for others, guys and girls alike.

Though at times everything within you wants to envy, be rude, or keep score, I challenge you to give and receive love! Whatever situation you face, love is the answer.

Jesus, You are the ultimate magnet because You are love! You promised in the Bible, "The one who is in you is greater than the one who is in the world" (1 John 4:4). Make Your love toward others great in me! Break my heart of envy, rudeness, and scorekeeping so I can love others as You do. Transform me so that love naturally, beautifully pours out. I long to be magnetic, just as You are. Amen.

Adjusting Our Expectations

Making a Habit of Joy

Why does it always happen to me? She had been dumped…again. Lately, nothing seemed to go right. Cammie just wanted to know why. *I always get the worst of everything. Mean teachers, work on the weekends, and getting caught—even when I'm not doing anything wrong! I just wish for once things would go my way. Like they do for Olivia. She always gets what she wants! She's got the perfect family, the perfect wardrobe, and most of all, the perfect boyfriend! He would never break up with her. If I had her life—no, if I just had her boyfriend, then I'd be happy!*

Cammie struggled to get out of her fog. Trapped in her gloomy view, she saw her life only one way: nothing was right and everything was wrong. And this wasn't just about the breakup—Cammie seemed to shade all her conversations in gray.

Maybe you have a friend like Cammie—or maybe you are Cammie. Like one continual rainy day, pessimism saturates every aspect of your life.

I have to admit I've been caught in an Eeyore cycle myself at times. And while there isn't an *easy* way out, there is a way. It starts with realizing that unwavering joy can't come from an unpredictable boy. In fact, it can't come from anyone or anything other than Jesus. Consistent joy comes within reach only when we stop reaching for the wrong things.

Going on a Joy Hunt

How are you doing when it comes to spotting and living in joy? Take the joy quiz.

A) You didn't get the role you wanted in the school play. You...
   1. are extremely depressed and determine to never try out again.
   2. become angry at God and pout for a week.
   3. trust God knows what He is doing and look for His good.

B) When you want to feel joyful, you...
   1. make plans for the weekend.
   2. go to the mall.
   3. carve out time with Jesus.

As an attribute of the fruit of the Holy Spirit, joy flows out of a heart filled with Him. He wants us to experience the fullest possible amount of His joy. Jesus made this clear in a prayer to His father: "I am coming to you now, but I say these things while I am still in the world, so that they may have the full measure of my joy within them" (John 17:13). Jesus didn't want His disciples, or us, to experience just a smidgen of joy. He wants us to overflow with it. Smiles, laughter...joy you can see!

C) Feeling sad, you...
1. are tempted to smoke or swig something.
2. make an ice-cream run.
3. pour worship music into your broken heart.

D) Seeing another person bubbling with joy, you...
1. find a way to shut her down.
2. are annoyed by her happiness.
3. want to be like her.

How did you do when it comes to joy?

10–12 points: You are well on your way to gaining joy's magnetic qualities.

7–9 points: Looks like you need some help finding joy.

4–6 points: Let's learn what joy is and get it!

Be sure to record your score in the back of the book, so you can identify your strengths as well as the areas where you need to seek God's help.

But how do we find joy in Someone we can't touch or see? How do we get out of the gunk of our less-than-perfect lives and get into this joy Jesus promised?

The answer comes with deciding to look for joy now rather than focusing on what seems to be missing. When Cammie looked at her life, she didn't see anything good because she couldn't see past the bad. She couldn't see joy because she didn't know where to find it.

HAPPY DOESN'T JUST HAPPEN; JOY TAKES ACTION

Take a second and look back over the questions in the quiz. Reread the questions. Can you see that each answer is linked to a decision? That's because our joy is determined by our choices, by how we choose to respond when life doesn't go our way. Joy begins with a decision to take action and go after it.

Maybe we're impacted by the movies we watch or songs we hear; whatever the reason, we tend to think the happy life just happens. Joy comes to us…someday…when our dreams come true. When we make the play, hit the homer, get the career, live at the beach—and get the guy. And when our dreams aren't fulfilled? We've hit bad luck or fate is against us. We deserve to be happy!

But our lives are not movies, running according to a script where things go our way if we just stay true to our dreams.

The truth is, joy is not waiting somewhere out there. It's right here within our reach—if we're willing to do the hard work of choosing it.

Joyful people make hard decisions and then do the hard work of shifting perspective instead of taking the easier route of soaking in self. Our minds tells us, *I deserve to feel sad,* and that's where we can get stuck. Do we really want to stay there, sad and bummed out? Or do we want joy? If so, that's gained through the choices we make. Because happy doesn't just happen; joy takes action.

KICK THE MISERY HABIT

So first, let's honestly ask ourselves, *Do I want joy?* I know it seems like a no-duh question, but sometimes I really think our silent answer is no. Think of that girl who talks nonstop about her troubles, the one who, when you talk about something hard in your life, always has to one-up you with her bigger problem. Sadness is the outfit she wears every day; she's absolutely miserable. Does she really want to be joyful? Or does she—do we—really just want attention?

Sometimes we become friends with our joyless hearts; we get comfortable. We need to take a good long look in the mirror and ask, *Do I want joy?* I didn't make up this seemingly obvious question.

Jesus did.

In John 5, Jesus was on His way to Jerusalem for a huge celebration. After entering the city, He saw a man suffering from illness. "When Jesus saw him lying there and learned that he had been in this condition for a long time, he asked him, 'Do you want to get well?'" (John 5:6).

Of course he wanted to get well! Why the question?

Recently, my tooth really ached. Even though it hurt, I kept rubbing my tongue over and over the sore. Why didn't I leave it alone? Why, even though it caused me pain, did I keep doing what made it hurt all the more?

I've done the same to the sore places on my heart. Replaying over and over the painful words he said or the promise she broke. I've poked at my anxiety, trust issues, worry, insecurity, loneliness, jealousy, sadness, and negativity. Jesus asks me, "Lynn, do you want to get well? Do you want to have joy?"

We may say we don't want these troubles in our lives, but the way we talk, think, and tell others about them suggests these issues are our friends!

Maybe you've grown so used to your issues, you can't imagine your life without anxiety, worry, or stress. "It's just who I am; I can't do anything about it."

Are you ready to get rid of being miserable or complaining so you can get beautiful? A hard question, but one we need to honestly answer.

For the invalid in John 5, misery had become a way of life. He'd been lying there for over thirty-eight years. But then Jesus told him, "Get up! Pick up your mat and walk!" (verse 8). Putting faith in Jesus, he got up. His actions showed he wanted to get well. The Bible says, "At once the man was cured; he picked up his mat and walked" (verse 9). He took action! He picked up the mat of his problem and walked away from it.

After the invalid was well, Jesus commanded, "See, you are well again. Stop sinning or something worse may happen to you" (verse 14).

Jesus can bring joy into our lives, but only we can decide to pick up our mat to get it. We have to kick the habit of complaining, moping, pouting by making up our minds to not be the downer in our day.

While Cammie wanted joy, drowning in self-pity wasn't going to get her there! She needed to stop wallowing in her sorrows and start doing the hard stuff: choosing uplifting songs instead of sappy ones, making friends who find happiness in Jesus rather than in substances, avoiding places that stir up sadness. She needed to hang out where joy hangs out.

JOY IS ATTRACTIVE

In the middle of making good but hard choices, Luke not only found joy, but he also found a joyful girl too! "I really wanted more of God in my life. I was experiencing Him in very intimate and powerful ways in prayer, worship, and studying the Bible. Thinking I would be distracted from growing closer to God, I set my mind to not date when I got to Auburn University. My perspective quickly changed! Across the room at a prayer meeting, I saw an absolutely beautiful girl with artistic clothes and trendy glasses. I heard her talk with God as a daughter would talk with her father. I just had to get to know her!"

Luke discovered his first impressions were right as he got to know this girl better. "Alison's heart for a deep, rich, and vibrant relationship with Jesus was extremely attractive to me. I wanted to hear her voice and learn about her passions, perspectives, and journey with God. Her sweet but blazing love for Jesus, along with her effortless beauty, caused me to want to get to know her more! She was living a joyful and purposeful life because of her love for Jesus. It was beautiful!"

Because Luke was pursuing a deeper relationship with Jesus, he was captivated upon finding a joy-filled girl doing the same!

Another guy I spoke with, Robbie, described a similar experience: "I was talking to this girl I met at Young Life, a Christian organization for teenagers. She was the most gorgeous girl I'd ever met. At camp, I saw her fall on her knees, worshiping God with her whole heart. This gesture showed how much she loved God; she didn't care if anyone made fun of her. To me, that is the most attractive thing a girl has ever done. That's the type of girl I've been looking for."

As guys pursuing Jesus, Robbie and Luke had several things in common:

- They found a girl pursuing Jesus attractive.
- They deliberately chose to hang out with people finding happiness in Jesus.
- They recognized and appreciated genuine joy when they spotted it.

Both Robbie and Luke were attracted to girls who reflected joy through their actions. Even a simple smile can show off joy in a heart. Parker said, "A smile is something that never gets old! A girl smiling causes me to notice her. You can never be too cool to wear a smile."

LOOKING FOR JOY MAKERS

Of course, our lives are going to have hard times in them—it's just part of living on this planet. Yet as we become the girl He wants, we can mature to the point where we can experience joy even in the hard times. Maturity like this is only developed by making the difficult choices that take us in joy's direction. One step on the right path is getting away from joy takers and getting around joy makers.

This is exactly what Nehemiah had to do.

You'll find his story in the Old Testament book that shares his name. He was living among his fellow Israelites in the foreign country of Babylon, after they'd been taken captive from their homeland. God had allowed this to happen because they had chosen joy fillers instead of the Filler of Joy. God had told them from the very beginning of their relationship that if they put joy fillers—or idols, as He called them—first, life would not go as they expected.

Doing what was right in their own eyes landed the Israelites in misery in a foreign land, exiled to Babylon for seventy years. Miserable, they cried out to God, "Get us out of here!" Miraculously He answered.

Nehemiah, employed by the Babylonian king, remained in Babylon while some of the Israelites returned to Jerusalem. His countrymen sent him a sad report after arriving in their native land: much of Jerusalem was in ruins (1:3). The Babylonians had torn down their homes and destroyed the temple where they worshiped.

Devastated by this news, Nehemiah decided not to just sit around and soak in depression but to take action. He pleaded with the king to let him go and help repair Jerusalem. The king granted his request (2:3–9).

For his mission, Nehemiah surrounded himself with true friends who loved God: joy makers. After surveying the mess, they got busy working to repair Jerusalem's walls (2:17–18).

Right in the middle of doing the work God had called them to do, the joy drainers showed up, guys with terrific names like Sanballat, Tobiah, and Geshem. Mocking and ridiculing, they asked, "What is this you are doing?" (2:19). (Don't you just love when you are doing exactly what God wants you to and someone comes along and puts you down?) Nehemiah kept right on doing the assignment God had given him; he refused to be distracted.

But the joy drainers didn't just show up once; they kept coming back. Again and again, Nehemiah and those with him had to ignore these joy takers; they had to do the hard stuff of choosing to put their focus on God.

Nehemiah knew that the key to getting and keeping joy is to keep right on doing what God has called you to do. Don't give joy drainers an ounce of your effort! Nehemiah didn't, and as a result, he and God's people reached their goal in record time! Ignoring the discouraging comments and working with all their heart, they repaired Jerusalem's huge stone walls in just fifty-two days (6:15)!

WONDERFUL WORDS OF JOY

When the job of rebuilding the wall was completed, the Israelites got ready to party! Bringing their favorite foods, they gathered together to be in God's presence and read His Word. "Nehemiah said, 'Go and enjoy choice food and sweet drinks, and send some to those who have nothing prepared. This day is sacred to our Lord. Do not grieve, for the joy of the LORD is your strength'" (8:10).

What did Nehemiah credit as the source of the people's strength? Joy! Unlikely, but powerful! "So the people went away to eat and drink at a festive meal, to share gifts of food, and to celebrate with great joy because they had heard God's words and understood them" (8:12, NLT).

Our God loves to celebrate and His words started a party! Knowing God's words brought powerful joy!

Really? you might be thinking. *That's all you've got?*

You feel let down? Did you expect some other secret? Something monumental?

God's Word is monumental! The Bible is packed with powerful truths and promises that bring joy when we know them! But first, we've got to get under the influence of God's Word! First Chronicles 16:27 says, "Splendor and majesty are before him; strength and joy in his dwelling place."

Reaching down to the innermost parts of our heart, soul, and mind, God's words give us strength and joy. "I will be glad and rejoice in your love," David wrote, "for you saw my affliction and knew the anguish of my soul" (Psalm 31:7).

In Psalm 31:7, where did David say he got his joy from?

. . . .

. . . .

Just out of high school, I was boyfriendless (I know, that isn't a word, but it fits perfectly!). My boyfriend and I had just broken up, and I was choosing to be miserable. I struggled to figure out who I was without a guy and wound up convincing myself I'd never find someone who was like me.

Nothing good comes of basing your identity on a guy. Boyfriend-based identity crumbles with a breakup.

Then some friends showed me two verses in Hosea that were just what I needed: "I will make you my wife forever, showing you righteousness and justice, unfailing love and compassion. I will be faithful to you and make you mine, and you will finally know me as the LORD" (2:19–20, NLT).

Boyfriend-based identity crumbles with a breakup.

At eighteen, I wasn't looking to get married, but I was really lonely. A thousand miles from home, I found that not having a boyfriend made me lonelier. I wrote out Hosea 2:19–20 on an index card and took it with me everywhere. During class, between classes, after class: I read it, read it, and read it some more. Knowing God was crazy about me brought me His joy!

GOING AFTER JOY MEANS GOING AFTER GOD

It's so easy to base our expectations for joy on something, someplace, or someone. And while they may bring short-term happiness, they never lead to long-term joy. The only place to find lasting joy is in God. That's why God told the Israelites in this story to get busy rebuilding the temple, so they could be with Him! He knows that when we look for joy in Him, we find it!

The Israelites of Nehemiah's day started off in the right direction, looking to God for joy. But somewhere along the way, they took a wrong turn. Even though it had not been that long since they'd returned from their exile in Babylon—the country they'd been defeated by as a result of not pursuing God first—they again forgot to make God their first priority. Caught up in rebuilding their own houses, wardrobes, and pantries, they left the temple, His house, in ruins.

God wasn't happy with their choice.

In fact, He got a little sarcastic: "Is it a time for you yourselves to be living in your paneled houses, while this house remains a ruin?" (Haggai 1:4). I can hear God: "Really? You just can't find the time to work on My house? You have plenty of time to do what you want to do." The temple in ruins spoke loud and clear about what was most important to them. They'd decided that looking out for their own interests was the way to get joy.

But as God pointed out, their plan for happiness wasn't working! "Give careful thought to your ways. You have planted much, but have harvested little. You eat, but never have enough. You drink, but never have your fill. You put on clothes, but are not warm. You earn wages, only to put them in a purse with holes in it" (verses 5–6).

They planted everything right, so why didn't their crops turn out?

The food was great, so why didn't they feel satisfied after eating?

Why weren't they cozy when they put on their favorite sweatshirt?

Why did their money slip away faster than they could save it?

The answer might surprise you. *God* had something to do with it. Check out verse 9: " 'You expected much, but see, it turned out to be little. What you brought home, I blew away. Why?' declares the LORD Almighty. 'Because of my house, which remains a ruin, while each of you is busy with his own house.' "

They'd been looking in the wrong place for joy. God wanted them to remember joy is found in Him!

We have a lot in common with the Israelites, looking everywhere but to Him for our joy:

If only I had more friends, then I'd be happy.

If only that guy would pay more attention to me, then I will feel wanted.

If only I were more athletic, then I could be proud.

If only I were thinner in that place and bigger in the other, then I'd be happy with myself.

By focusing on the "if onlys," we miss the joy we can experience right here, right now in God: "The ransomed of the LORD will return. They will enter Zion with singing; everlasting joy will crown their heads. Gladness and joy will overtake them, and sorrow and sighing will flee away" (Isaiah 35:10).

Joy will overtake them? I want to be overtaken with joy! David tells us how: "You have made known to me the path of life; you will fill me with joy in your presence, with eternal pleasures at your right hand" (Psalm 16:11).

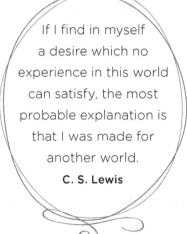

If I find in myself a desire which no experience in this world can satisfy, the most probable explanation is that I was made for another world.

C. S. Lewis

We choose joy when we choose Him! We put ourselves in a place to get joy when we choose to be with God, when we spend time talking to Him as we would our best friend, when we read His Word as eagerly as a text from a crush. Listen to what happened to David's heart as he spent time with God:

You did it: You turned my deepest pains into joyful dancing; You stripped off my dark clothing and covered me with joyful light.

You have restored my honor. My heart is ready to explode, erupt in
new songs! It's impossible to keep quiet! Eternal One, my God,
my Life-Giver, I will thank You forever. (Psalm 30:11–12, VOICE)

Maybe you're reading this saying, "But you don't know my life; there
is absolutely nothing to be joyful about!" Remember, joy begins with a
choice. The 180-degree turn David experienced from pain to dancing
came with choosing to find joy in God.

I don't believe in Three Easy Steps to the Perfect Life, but I do know
finding joy begins with you going after it!

Begin at the beginning: Give all of you for all of Him. Stop holding
out on God. You won't find joy if on Sunday you claim His way is the best
way but on Monday you look to a boy!

You will get as much of God as you want. Want His best? Give Him
your best!

AVOID JOY DRAINERS

One way we give God our best is when we direct our thoughts toward
Him. Too often we let our minds drift and then stick on the wrong
people, the wrong places, and the wrong things. We get stuck…spinning
and spinning while our joy drains.

Getting caught up in other people's drama can definitely send our
thoughts spiraling. King David experienced the full effect when joy
drainers got to him. Check out his desperate prayer:

Have mercy on me, LORD, for I am in distress. Tears blur my
eyes. My body and soul are withering away. I am dying from
grief; my years are shortened by sadness. Sin has drained my
strength; I am wasting away from within. I am scorned by all

my enemies and despised by my neighbors—even my friends are afraid to come near me. When they see me on the street, they run the other way. (Psalm 31:9–11, NLT)

 What is one noun you would use to describe the source of David's pain as he spelled it out in Psalm 31:9–11?

. . . .
. . . .

The one word I'd use to describe David's distress is *people.* Enemies, neighbors, friends—joy drainers who strategically ridiculed, avoided, and wore him out.

Are other people draining your joy too? Friends, family, schoolmates wrapped up in drinking, drugs, drama with guys?

Or maybe your joy drainers are places. School, work, even home sometimes! *If I could just get out of here!* Life is hard; there's just no way of getting around that. Sitting in school when it's gorgeous outside, your parents' fight still ringing in your ears. Watching the scoreboard as it trumpets your team's loss—again.

Maybe your struggle is in comparing your life to others' or in buying the lies they've used against you: "One time won't hurt." "You're missing out." "You're dumb to be such a prude."

Now you know they were wrong and you were right. But you've lost your joy because you've lost yourself. And you believe it's too late to get it back now.

It's not too late! Don't buy that lie! You can choose to walk away from them and walk toward Him.

What joy drainer do you need to walk away from? A boyfriend, a job, a team? Maybe you need to stop putting yourself down, comparing yourself to other people, weighing yourself every day. Stop letting that guy use you, stop turning to substances to make you forget or fit in, stop working so hard to look perfect.

And then you need to take action: move toward God to get His joy.

FOCUS ON JOY MAKERS

Whether your joy was stolen by people, places, or the pursuit of worthless things, God specializes in restoring hope. If you will take your joyless, broken heart and give it to Him, He will repair it! Jesus died so that you could be whole. He'll take away your anger, bitterness, and brokenness and fill those empty spaces with Himself.

And once He brings healing to our hearts, we have to get off the mat of our issues and walk, just like the invalid healed by Jesus. Here's our "Get up!" command: "Give thanks to the LORD, call on his name; make known among the nations what he has done" (1 Chronicles 16:8).

Praising God and giving Him thanks is our direction to get joy! Centering our thoughts on thankfulness helps protect us from joy drainers. Studies show that thankful people are happier people.[1] So practice expressing gratitude for all God has done for you.

I loved what Madi said to me this morning: "Absolutely nothing makes me happier than talking about Jesus!" Just sharing about His goodness with another person takes the power away from joy-robbing circumstances and sets your heart and mind on good! Boldness is beautiful!

Another way I fill my thoughts with joy is to keep God's Word close by. Here are a few of my favorites:

Bring joy to your servant, for to you, O Lord, I lift up my soul.
(Psalm 86:4)

Satisfy us in the morning with your unfailing love, that we may sing for joy and be glad all our days. (Psalm 90:14)

In the multitude of my anxieties within me, Your comforts delight my soul. (Psalm 94:19, NKJV)

Just speaking out loud these powerful reminders redirects my heart. You may want to put these on your phone, in your purse, or on your mirror to protect yourself against a possible joy robbery! You might even tweet them!

Whatever you do, make a choice to move your thoughts away from joy robbers and center them on Jesus. If your joy robber is being boyfriendless, don't allow your life to be all wrapped up in finding "the one"! Joy comes to those who focus on loving the One, Jesus. Seek Him—not him!

Parker offered this piece of advice: "Enjoy being single; use that time to love yourself and grow deeper in love with Jesus. Don't fall into the trap of thinking, *I'm the only single girl in my class, so I just need to get a boyfriend.* That's how hearts get broken. There are tons of godly dudes out there; trust God that He has one picked out when the time is right."

Don't hang your joy on waiting for "the one." Seek Him—not him!

Luke had a similar suggestion: "Give Jesus the desires of your heart. Abandon what you want to Him. Choose to deeply love Him before deeply loving a guy. Meet Jesus in your prayers, your worship, your thoughts, and study His promises often. Develop an intimacy with Him that will be a natural place for you to become more like Him."

What great advice! We often forget that Jesus was joyful during His time on earth. Even though He knew that His future was to die for us, He chose joy because His death meant we could be with Him forever. As the writer of Hebrews says, "Because of the joy awaiting him, he endured the cross, disregarding its shame. Now he is seated in the place of honor beside God's throne" (12:2, NLT).

Jesus, more than anyone else, understood that joy is not found in our circumstances but in our relationship with the Father. There is also no one as magnetic as Jesus. Everywhere He went, He drew a crowd. People just wanted to be near Him.

So let's choose to let His joy shine through us!

Jesus, today I choose to stop fixating on joy drainers. I choose to focus on the joy of You by reading Your love letter to me and getting around joy makers. Make me magnetic, Jesus! Amen.

Drop the Drama

Pursuing Peace

No one could get away with treating her that way! Tammy had been flirting with Andie's boyfriend all week; she wasn't putting up with it any more. Andie told Tammy to back off, but she just wasn't getting it. She didn't care if the whole school witnessed the scene—she'd show Tammy not to mess with her guy!

Few things can make a girl lose it faster than a flirting friend. Even so, drama never looks good on a girl, and something tells me Andie's boyfriend doesn't find this drama attractive either!

Andie needs to get a grip. In the heat of the moment, peace might seem impossible, but it *is* possible. Andie can find harmony and tranquility—even with Tammy!

I'm guessing Andie has experienced the adrenaline rush of drama, the enjoyment of grabbing everyone's attention just at the right time. It's easy to transform a quick glance from an old friend into an evil glare—that story is so much better!

Stirring up trouble can be addictive, a thrill in getting others emotionally worked up. What a dangerous pattern! We can grow so used to the attention we get from spinning a story that we can start to crave this attention, even if it is a bit warped.

You might be thinking, *How does she know?* Well, I'm a girl!

Are You Making Peace or Waging War?

Add up your score on this quiz and compare it to the scale at the end:

A) Bathing-suit pictures on Facebook are driving you crazy. You...
1. comment rudely on them.
2. unfriend them.
3. block them.

B) For the third time this week, your best friend texted you in the middle of the night. You...
1. tell her to stop bugging you.
2. respond each time but make her feel your frustration.
3. kindly say, "I love you, but I need my sleep!"

When I began my journey of wanting to become magnetic, I started a new pattern. Becoming the girl He wants meant I needed to choose carefully how I worded a story, who to tell, what to tell, and when to tell it. Exaggerating to make the story more interesting, drawing in others' sympathy, or sharing a hurtful comment overheard all tend to separate friends. When choosing peace, we choose to consistently and intention-ally think about our words. That's when others can feel safe to pursue a

C) Day after day you hear stories from the girl who allows a guy to use her. You...
  1. show how disgusted you are by her choices.
  2. find a new place to eat your lunch.
  3. look for opportunities to share her true worth with her.
D) Your brother and sister are fighting again. You...
  1. scream "Knock it off!"
  2. ignore them.
  3. help them work it out.

How did you do? If you got...
  10-12 points: You're using the power of peace!
  7-9 points: Sometimes you give peace a chance.
  4-6 points: You're in need of a drama diet!
  Don't forget to record your score in the back of the book, so you can identify your strengths as well as the areas where you need to seek God's help.

deeper relationship with us. Proverbs 11:25 says, "He who refreshes others will himself be refreshed."

And peace is definitely attractive. You might think guys only notice a girl's outward appearance, but I've found godly guys look further than the face. Listen to how Kent describes the peace he spotted in Becky the first time he saw her:

"I'd been invited by a mutual friend to join Becky's family for dinner. The first time I saw her, she was descending the stairs in her parents' home. All I could think was, *Beautiful. Radiant. Wholesome.*

"I quickly realized Becky wasn't like what I *thought* I wanted in life," he continued. "I had been attracted to the blond-cheerleader, soccer-player type girl—the ones the guys were fighting over. Through spending time with many of these girls, though, I had discovered some were superficial, with most of their time caught up in drama and gossip. Becky was different—peaceful and quiet.

"While my first thought about her was, *How gorgeous!* even more than that I recognized Becky's incredible poise. Gracious. Calming. Godly. Although she was the opposite of my hypersocial, always go-go-go personality, I felt at home with her."

Just reading Kent's description of Becky makes me feel peaceful! No wonder he thought she was gorgeous!

Take the quiz on pages 46–47 to see how you're doing when it comes to giving peace a chance to make you gorgeous!

The Drama Diet: Developing a Taste for Peace

A drama diet involves choosing peace rather than emotions as the driver in our lives. Like eating junk food, living on drama leaves us craving more; peace, however, is incredibly satisfying.

Grabbing an apple rather than chips takes discipline; so does choosing peace. As one girl I know asked, "If we don't talk about other girls, what are we supposed to talk about?" The switch from dramatic to peaceful comes through daily choices that stretch us, sometimes painfully so! Ignoring a hurtful comment on Instagram. Speaking truth when your emotions want to blow up. Finding a positive solution instead of echoing the chorus of complaints. Whatever the situation, we can follow David's advice: "Turn from evil and do good; seek peace and pursue it" (Psalm 34:14).

Can you hear God's challenge to us? Go after peace. Accepting this challenge begins with obedience. Obedience, especially when it goes against our screaming emotions, can be extremely hard. In fact, we might even think, *Why should I have to learn this hard stuff? Why do I need to be peaceful while everyone else blows up at every little thing?*

Ever tried to sign up for a class at school when you noticed the little asterisk after the description? Looking below you notice a footnote: you must take Multimedia 101 before signing up for this class. There is a prerequisite to get into the more advanced computer class—passing 101.

Sometimes getting God's best in every area of our lives comes with some prerequisites. Passing Obedience 101 is one of those. God needs you to learn to say yes to Him now so that when bigger issues come up, with bigger blessings in the balance, you'll have already learned to obey. Your new level of trust, gained through obedience, helps you to trust Him with even bigger things. That's the preparation you need to handle His bigger blessings!

Choosing peace over drama is one area we need to learn obedience, and learning obedience can be really hard—at least it is for me!

I did it again. Stepped into a situation that didn't concern me. I told myself I was helping, but it wasn't my problem. As usual, my efforts backfired.

How did that happen? How did I manage to mess up when I was just trying to help?

Here Jesus spoke to me. Of course, not literally *spoke to me,* but He nudged my heart: *You're a meddler, Lynn, and you need to be done with it. When you meddle, you're not trusting. When you meddle, you're saying that I can't handle it. You know I can.*

A meddler? Really, God? What is a meddler anyway? I actually looked it up. A meddler is someone who interferes without a right or an invitation, who gets involved when she's not wanted. He didn't call me a fixer. I wish He had; that doesn't sound so bad. No, I'm not a fixer. But I'm definitely not a gossiper either; my heart is never to *intentionally* separate people. I want to help. Really I do.

And that's where I get into trouble. Seeing an unhappy, unhealthy, or unholy situation, I listen to the whisper in my head. Since I *see* it, I think I'm supposed to do something about it. I let go of my peace and get involved. Not smart. First Thessalonians 4:11 says, "Aspire to live quietly, and to mind your own affairs, and to work with your hands, as we instructed you" (ESV).

My place is to be quiet and pray.

Ask Jesus for prayers to pray, not words to say.

Now that I see my actions for what they are, it's my responsibility to change. To change, I have to slow down before I open my mouth. I have to ask myself, *Am I meddling?*

Will I be tempted to interfere, to get involved when I shouldn't? Every day! Will I mess up? I hope not, but it's highly probable. I'm human. My desire, though, is to mind my own business and let Jesus do His work. I will ask for prayers to pray, not words to say.

Change is hard. But I know Jesus is serious about us not meddling.

Proverb 26:17 says, "Whoever meddles in a quarrel not his own is like one who takes a passing dog by the ears" (ESV). Not wise and not attractive!

Can you think of times when you got involved though you shouldn't have? When Jesus simply wanted you to find His peace in the situation? To pray and only pray?

When we don't respond in situations peacefully, God's way, we're choosing to sin. Like me when I meddle. Sin is the ultimate peace stealer. In fact, sin eventually leaves us downright miserable. When we choose to go against God's way, we walk away from peace and right into trouble. The drama diet helps us go God's way.

OPEN UP OR COVER UP?

When on a drama diet, we must decide the wisest way to handle occasions when someone offends us. Social media is an open invitation to tell everyone everything, whether or not they want to hear it! The Holy Spirit rarely inspires us to share in public something hurtful that happened in private. At times, however, He prompts us to have a conversation with the person who hurt us so we can move toward forgiveness and healing.

Proverbs 17:9 tells us, "He who covers over an offense promotes love, but whoever repeats the matter separates close friends."

When you feel aggravated, do you find it easier to open up, by talking over the problem with the offender, or to cover up, by simply moving on? Why?

. . . .

. . . .

. . . .

. . . .

When trying to decide if it's wiser to open up or cover up, begin by asking yourself, *Does this conversation need to take place in order to...*

1. *keep the relationship?*
2. *be sure nothing comes between us?*
3. *get it off my chest?*

If you answered yes to 1 and 2, it's probably time for a peaceful talk with the person involved. If your answer to 3 is yes, it's time for a talk... with the Holy Spirit! Ask Him to give you His perspective before you take your next step.

Too often, our natural tendency is to give the other person what we think he deserves. God asks us to seek peace in our own words and actions—no matter how the other person acts. In Romans 12:17–19 Paul instructs us,

> Do not repay anyone evil for evil. Be careful to do what is right in the eyes of everybody. If it is possible, as far as it depends on you, live at peace with everyone. Do not take revenge, my friends, but leave room for God's wrath, for it is written: "It is mine to avenge; I will repay," says the Lord.

After we have done as much as we can, we have to let go and allow Jesus to take care of our troubles!

Those of us wired for confrontation might really struggle here. We justify our behavior by saying, "It's just the way I am. I can't let things go." We use our natural boldness to excuse the ways we stir up trouble rather than smoothing things over. But Proverbs 17:19 tells us, "He who loves a quarrel loves sin; he who builds a high gate invites destruction." We have to switch our script from "It's just the way I am" to "God, refine who I am."

No One Is Pretty When They're Dripping

I love falling asleep to the sound of rain. The peaceful, steady downpour lulls me to relax. One night I drifted off to Slumberland to the tune of summer rain. When...

Drip. Drip. Drip. Again and again, a single drop plunked onto the exercise mat across the room. Slumberland became Psycholand as I stormed out of bed, irritated and annoyed. *Why does this stuff always happen to me?* I was on the verge of blowing up. Focusing my sleep-filled eyes, I floundered to the garage, yanked a bucket off the shelf, and threw it under the noisy dribble. *Plop. Plop. Plop.* Now raindrops splattered into the bucket.

Believe me, there was nothing attractive about me or my attitude that night. Given a choice, no one would put themselves in a room with a dripping roof.

Given a choice, no guy would put himself with a dripping girl either. That's how the Bible describes the person who stirs up strife, driving guys away:

A quarrelsome wife is like a constant dripping. (Proverbs 19:13)

Better to live on a corner of the roof than share a house with a quarrelsome wife. (Proverbs 21:9)

I know, these verses are written for wives, which doesn't apply to you now. But your choices today shape the woman you'll be tomorrow. Who do you want to be? Known as the one everyone wants to be around, or as a person continually picking fights or complaining?

But what about when my best friend lets my secrets slip or my boyfriend makes plans with his friends instead of me? Confrontation seems the logical response! You want them to know exactly how you feel, and you want to them to know now! You've got two choices:

Door Number 1: peace, responding calmly when needed and
    letting it go when not

Door Number 2: returning fire, sending a clear message so
    they'll never treat you that way again

Initially, it may feel powerful to let your frustration fly, but that's letting someone else determine how you behave and feel. If you go through Door Number 2, your friend, boyfriend, or enemy knows exactly how to get a reaction from you.

Peace is the power choice of the magnetic girl.

Choosing Door Number 1, pursuing peace *before* you pop, keeps you in control.

Peace is your power choice. *Any* girl can tell someone off, making a friend feel awful while temporarily making herself feel good. Blowing up is the common response. You can become magnetic by tapping into the power of the Holy Spirit and doing the opposite, choosing peace instead.

TRAIN YOUR BRAIN

Of course, just knowing peace is the power choice doesn't make it easy. We have to practice making this power choice if we want the fruit of the Spirit to thrive in our lives. That means retraining our brains to respond as Jesus wants rather than going with our natural tendencies.

Grab your highlighter and open your Bible to Philippians 4:6–9. Yes, I've written it out below, but this passage is one of those lifers—one you're going to need often, so you'll want to go ahead and mark it in your own Bible.

Go ahead. Get your Bible and look it up. I'll wait. ☺

What does Philippians 4:6-9 say we should be anxious for?

. . . .

. . . .

. . . .

Do not be anxious about anything, but in everything, by prayer and petition, with thanksgiving, present your requests to God. And the peace of God, which transcends all understanding, will guard your hearts and your minds in Christ Jesus. Finally, brothers, whatever is true, whatever is noble, whatever is right, whatever is pure, whatever is lovely, whatever is admirable—if anything is excellent or praiseworthy—think about such things. Whatever you have learned or received or heard from me, or seen in me—put it into practice. And the God of peace will be with you. (Philippians 4:6–9)

How does this passage tell us to get away from anxiety? Mark every helpful word or phrase you see in the passage above.

. . . .

. . . .

. . . .

. . . .

. . . .

If you're a lifeguard, work at a fitness center, or have taken a high-school health class, chances are you've learned about cardiopulmonary resuscitation (CPR). CPR is an emergency procedure preserving brain function and helping save the life of a person who is in cardiac arrest, meaning their heart has malfunctioned and stopped beating unexpectedly.

When you are upset and mad, your spiritual heart is under cardiac arrest. You need the CPR of Philippians 4:6–9:

- **C**hoose not to be anxious.
- **P**ray about everything.
- **R**emember to be thankful.

Three verbs, three actions you can take to get peace: Choose. Pray. Remember. When you feel your blood pressure rising, give yourself CPR!

Choosing Not to Be Anxious

What should I do now? Why did he say that? What did she really mean? Spinning round and round, our thoughts circle our problem until we're

The God who keeps the world spinning can take care of my spinning!

dizzy. Training our brains to go to Jesus stops the spinning. We place our hearts in the center of His peace when we literally stop what we are doing and ask for His wisdom. Getting God's perspective gives us the wise perspective.

God promises that when we ask for His wisdom, He will give it—and lots of it (James 1:5). We just have to make sure that when we ask, we want His answer and will then obey it!

The girl who trusts and relies on God is calm. She has assurance that the One who hangs the stars and raises the sun has her life under control.

She sets aside drama and worry, choosing instead to look at her problem and size it up against God's promises in His Word. I often quote Isaiah 26:3 to myself when my heart starts racing: "You will keep in perfect peace all who trust in you, all whose thoughts are fixed on you!" (NLT)

While you can't control what others say or how they behave, you can determine what you say and how you'll behave. You can't choose peace for other people, but you can choose peace for you! Hebrews 12:14 tells us, "Make every effort to live in peace with all men and to be holy; without holiness no one will see the Lord."

Pray About EVERYTHING

Praying about everything empowers us to stick with our plan for peace. You might ask, "But does God really care about everything?" Yes, He does! Not just big stuff, like getting an F on your final, your parents' divorce, or the breakup with your boyfriend. He cares where you left your cell phone too! Prayer can bring peace to every situation, no matter the size. When a guy sees you face tremendous turmoil or horrendous hair and neither freaks you out, that's attractive! Calm is cool!

Through prayer, we transfer pressure from ourselves to One who can do everything and anything! Who better to handle our problems than the capable Creator?

Sometimes the best thing to do is remove yourself from the difficult situation for a bit. This cooling-off period gives you time to get alone with God to pray. You might want to go for a run, letting off steam as you pray. Take a walk in your favorite quiet place, talking the problem over with Him. Even sink down into a bubble bath to relax alone with God. Madi shared with me, "When I get in God's presence through listening to worship music, I literally feel like all my troubles are gone. He really lifts my heart and gives me peace!"

Have you tried relieving stress by hitting a pillow? working out?

crying in your room? These are all ways to relieve pain, frustration, and anxiety. You may have tried unhealthy ways too: cutting, drinking, drugs, boys.

When the pressure of frustration, worry, or sadness builds up, crying out to God is the perfect way to relieve stress. Yell, scream, cry. He won't get mad or hold anything against you.

What people, places, or problems threaten to steal your peace? Describe your situation.

. . . .

. . . .

. . . .

. . . .

. . . .

Over and over in the Psalms we see how David took his troubles to God in prayer: "O Lord, how many are my foes! How many rise up against me!… Arise, O Lord! Deliver me, O my God! Strike all my enemies on the jaw; break the teeth of the wicked" (Psalm 3:1, 7).

Not all pretty and wrapped up in a pink bow, is it? David was gut honest with God: he was mad at the people who were making his life miserable. He knew to take his anger to God, who could do something about his issues. David looked to God for peace to still his swirling emotions:

But you are a shield around me, O Lord; you bestow glory on me and lift up my head. To the Lord I cry aloud, and he answers me from his holy hill…. I lie down and sleep; I wake again, because the Lord sustains me. I will not fear the tens of thousands drawn up against me on every side. (verses 3–6)

Shield, sleep, sustain—all words to calm my chaotic heart. This is the place I can go when my world is whirling. I don't have to let people, places, or problems push me around. I can gain strength and confidence no matter where I am. I can get His wisdom to help me peacefully face whatever or whoever I need to. I can speak calmly because I have dumped my anxiety on the One who can handle it instead of lashing out at those who can't.

Prayer delivers God's power to our problems.

 Do you have a relationship constantly on edge? Write a prayer for God's peace in the relationship.

. . . .

. . . .

. . . .

. . . .

. . . .

Remember to Be Thankful

When you're unloading your panicky prayers on God, add a bit of thankfulness to it: *God, thank You for my parents. I know they are a gift from You. Can You help me with this gift? It's driving me crazy!*

Thankfulness and peace go together. Remember what we read in our CPR passage: "In everything, by prayer and petition, with thanksgiving, present your requests to God" (Philippians 4:6).

Practice here. Start by telling God something you are thankful for and then add your request.

. . . .

. . . .

. . . .

. . . .

While God loves to hear us say "thank You," *we* are the true benefactors of our gratitude. Thankfulness moves us from complaining to contentment, empowering us to find good even in our less-than-perfect reality.

Put It All Together

In the next twenty-four hours, something or someone is going to try to steal your peace. Remember CPR: Choose. Pray. Remember.

This isn't easy stuff; in fact, training your brain takes a level of maturity you might not have right now. Consistently going to Jesus will strengthen your ability to find God's peace even in the darkest situations. Peace can be the new you—the magnetic girl who's easier to get along with!

TAKE THE PRESSURE OFF

Finding our peace and confidence in God not only takes the pressure off us, it also takes pressure off others. The weight of our happiness doesn't rest on them. They don't have to worry or struggle to constantly stay on our good side. The peaceful girl loosens up! As Payden said, "I like a girl who is ladylike, outgoing, and not afraid to be silly!"

Guys seem to be especially drawn to girls so at peace with themselves they aren't forcing a relationship or frantically trying to grab attention. "I like a girl who doesn't need to constantly text or connect through social media," Isaiah told me. "Guys like girls who are God sufficient, completely content in their relationship with God. They don't need a guy to make them happy."

Joshua gave me more insight on how a peaceful girl stands out from the crowd: "One of the best attributes of the fruit of the Spirit is peace, when someone is surrendered to Jesus. If you truly have peace in Christ, all the other fruits of the Spirit fall into place. The moment you grasp peace, you also gain contentment, whether or not you have a boyfriend or spouse. Trusting Jesus is key to this peace. I think females in general worry a lot, especially about not finding a godly guy."

Does that describe you? As a young woman, I constantly wondered if I'd find a guy like me who would like me. Worry consumed my thoughts and caused me to waste a lot of time and energy. Joshua seems to be saying it's all a waste anyway, since a girl who's worried about finding a guy is a turnoff.

By contrast, when Joshua found his wife, Samantha, he saw a peace in her. So I asked Samantha how she got to the place where she wasn't constantly consumed over worrying about a guy:

"Despite growing up in a home with parents who truly loved the Lord, I knew of God but didn't love God," Samantha shared. "That lack grew even deeper during college. Nothing satisfied me. Not bottles of beer, frat parties, or the arms of guys. My search included exercising several hours a day, fixing my hair just so, and hanging out with the 'right' people. Every spring-break trip, good grade, or purchase of brand-name clothing just left me in a slump after the temporary high.

"During these years," she continued, "I consistently felt a tug on my heart. When I was down or lonely, I would pick up my Bible and read. I'd pray while taking a jog around town. Occasionally I'd even go to church, but I always felt a great sadness. Looking back, I know my tears were the Holy Spirit in me grieving. I'd ask the Lord to forgive me; I'd even stay away from the parties, drinking, and guys for a few weeks. But eventually I'd start the cycle all over again."

Samantha's story reminds me of so many I've heard, of girls who long for peace but just can't seem to find it. Happily, hers doesn't end there:

"This lasted for many years until the guy I wanted to marry broke my heart. After dating almost a year, I expected a marriage proposal.

Instead he quit calling and coming around. I cried for months. One night I couldn't take it any longer. There had to be more than tears, frustrations, and blahs. The Bible told me there was only one hope: Jesus.

"I started reading the Bible and asked God to forgive me for running so far from Him. I began praying. I joined a church and small group, where we learned about Scripture, prayed for each other, and had fun!

"I realized the 'something' I was missing was a solid decision to follow Jesus. I hadn't allowed Him to be Lord over my life and every decision I made. I was like a boat without an anchor. When things got tough, I was a wreck and had no peace. That's why I turned to drinking and guys: to try to find satisfaction and self-worth in them. I really believe the fruit of the Spirit my husband, Josh, initially found attractive in me is a direct result of deciding to walk away from my sin and getting to know God."

Samantha finally found peace when she escaped the pressure of trying to steer life on her own, when she learned to get her needs met through God instead of guys. And that's exactly why Josh found her irresistibly magnetic!

PUTTING PEACE INTO PRACTICE

So now that we know where to go with our frustration, worry, and hurt, are you willing to step away from the drama to gain the peace you need? The answer depends on who you want to be: the girl continually wrapped up and dragged down by drama, or the girl full of peace?

I'm not always successful at going to Jesus instead of going after someone when I am upset, but when I do, I find peace and I live with fewer regrets. We can choose to filter our feelings through prayer instead of taking it out on someone. We'll need to say "I'm sorry" less often when we're on our knees instead of on the phone.

James 3:17–18 tells us, "But the wisdom from above is first of all pure. It is also peace loving, gentle at all times, and willing to yield to others. It is full of mercy and good deeds. It shows no favoritism and is always sincere. And those who are peacemakers will plant seeds of peace and reap a harvest of righteousness" (NLT).

When we get God's wisdom for our lives, He will point us to the peaceful way. When we plant peace in our relationships, eventually we will get peace in our hearts.

Jesus, peace is hard to grasp and hold on to, especially when so much of life is beyond my control. Help me filter my feelings through prayer. Help me practice the power choice of peace! Amen.

Wait Training 101

Exercises in Patience

Barely able to drag yourself up to the front porch of your house, you drop your bag and dig for your keys—only to realize you must have left them somewhere. So you bang on the door for someone to let you in. Eight hours of school plus three hours of basketball practice equals nothing but dead legs and a migraine. The door finally opens and a tornado blows past, barreling over your bag and smashing your throbbing feet. Your little sister is trying to tell you every detail from youth group, but she can't get through her story because she's laughing so hard. She goes on and on...and so does her energy.

She manages to drain the tiniest bit of life you have left. Aggravated, you lose that one strand of patience, yelling at her. "Calm down!" *Pop!* In one fell swoop you've burst her happy mood. Her heart, deflated, plummets to the ground.

You ignore her wounded expression and head off to crash in your room, wondering to yourself, *Why does she have to be so annoying?*

Annoying. That seems to be our favorite adjective to describe the people and situations we encounter every day.

The funny thing is, what I find annoying, another person finds funny. In fact, the silly jokes and constant laughter that sometimes drive you crazy may actually be attractive to someone else! Isaiah said, "I like when a girl can laugh, smile, and doesn't mind running in the rain and splashing in puddles for the sake of having fun!" Sounds like a girl who enjoys some lighthearted fun is magnetic!

What types of behavior do you find most annoying?

. . . .
. . . .
. . . .
. . . .
. . . .

Too often when I feel impatience, my first thought is, *What's their problem?* Maybe the problem isn't theirs.

Maybe it's mine.

In fact, when I'm easily annoyed, the book of Proverbs says I'm a fool.

A fool? That's not attractive! It's not what I want and not what God wants for me either!

The magnetic girl is no fool. She doesn't allow other people or circumstances to determine her mood. She lets annoying comments go and practices patience.

The very definition of *patience* challenges me: "calm endurance of hardship, delay, or annoyance without complaint, loss of temper, or irritation." Even when the light at the intersection has been red forever, or when I'm frustrated with a project because the WiFi is down!

Patience sets us apart from others. It's simply not "normal"!

Patience attracted Andrew to Amber, though he might not have put it in those words. "When I met Amber, she wasn't looking for somebody, so our relationship was entirely based on friendship. From the beginning, I knew she was someone very special."

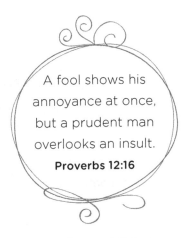

A fool shows his annoyance at once, but a prudent man overlooks an insult.
Proverbs 12:16

Amber's patience, shown by not chasing after a boyfriend, was attractive to Andrew. She wasn't pushing, trying to make something happen. She was simply herself, and that girl was gorgeous to Andrew.

"Amber was extremely easy to talk to and get along with," Andrew went on. "I think the ability to simply talk is often overlooked in the dating culture. If you are unable to simply have a conversation and share common interests, a dating relationship will probably not be very successful."

Andrew is right! The ability to simply talk with someone without dominating the conversation is often overlooked. I know when I'm talking or texting a friend or family member, I have so much to say! Minutes can go by—and I still haven't even given them a chance to say anything. It isn't a conversation; it's a play-by-play of my life. Guys are looking for girls who can have a dialogue, not give a monologue!

Conversing, both talking and listening without grabbing the first opportunity to jump in again, takes maturity and patience. But with texting and social media becoming the primary ways many of us communicate, these real communication skills are quickly becoming a lost art. This is another chance for you to stand out from the masses.

When questions linger—*Does he like me? What can I do to get him to notice me? Should I text him or just give him my number?*—it's so easy to try to nudge things along with a little tweet or text. But the magnetic girl knows that hurrying things often isn't wise!

Is Patience a Virtue for You?

Let's measure how you are doing on your wait training with a patience pop quiz:

A) You need supper in a hurry to get to practice on time. Your mom is running late. You say...

    1. "Why isn't my food ready?"

    2. "Give me money to eat out."

    3. "How can I help?"

B) Your parents' rule is no dating until you're sixteen. You...

    1. sneak behind their back—you just can't wait any more.

    2. obey but complain about their rules.

    3. wait patiently for the big day.

C) You check your grades online and find your teacher is not up to date. You...

    1. send her multiple e-mails and keep asking, wearing her down.

Go ahead and strike up a conversation. Introduce yourself and talk to him. But be patient; let him take it from there!

That's what Amber did, and it certainly got Andrew's attention. "Being patient and trusting in God is essential when finding someone truly

2. ask her twice about your grade
   at the next class period.
3. e-mail her and ask for your
   current grade.

D) You pick up your friend for school each morning. She is consistently two to three minutes
late. You...

1. tell her she needs to find
   another ride.
2. begin texting her your exact
   arrival time each day, hoping
   she'll get the hint.
3. enjoy your music until she's ready.

How did you do? If you got...

10–12 points: Your trying is paying off!

7–9 points: Time to make your patience workout a priority.

4–6 points: You're in need of a patience coach!

Don't forget to record your score in the back of
the book, so you can identify your strengths as well
as the areas where you need to seek God's help.

Text or tweet? Neither. Start a conversation in person; let him make the next move!

special," he told me. "I feel God was preparing me as well as Amber for the time when we were truly ready for a relationship.

"Patience is so important. I saw that in Amber. God doesn't make mistakes. Romans 8:28 says, 'And we know that in all things God works for the good of those who love him, who have been called according to his purpose.' This verse implies that waiting is not passive, but active."

Andrew wrapped up with this challenge to others: "Prepare yourself, keep pure, be in prayer, and have healthy friendships with people of the opposite sex while keeping your purity, both physical and emotional."

Wait. Let God Orchestrate.

No place does the waiting game play out more obviously than with guys. Our hearts started crushing on little boys back in third grade. (Or was that just me?) Starting so young makes waiting seem worse!

That's where the magnetic girl is different. She knows God wants us to wait and let Him orchestrate.

Isaiah put it this way: "Part of being a man is pursuing the beauty. Let him make most of the advances; God wired him to have great joy in pursuing you. Seek to spend time with him and just be his friend. If he's who God wants you to be with, he'll notice you."

Guys want to chase. Give them something to chase! They don't need or want too much information too fast. Take your time showing a guy you like him. You can wait for God's best and God's timing.

When you meet a cute guy, what kind of questions run through your mind? What do you do with these questions?

. . . .
. . . .
. . . .
. . . .
. . . .
. . . .

A girl who endures waiting without growing agitated and annoyed is uncommon in our culture. Most of us are used to having everything we want even before we want it, so we tend to think waiting is a waste.

But is it?

Waiting's a waste when our impatience brews, but waiting's magnetic when patience blooms. Proverbs 14:29 says, "A patient man has great understanding, but a quick-tempered man displays folly."

Andrew explained why patience is so important when it comes to relationships: "The very core should be Jesus Christ. Knowing Amber loves the same Jesus I do and knowing He is at the center of our relationship makes our relationship easier and great! I am grateful God saved me from meeting Amber until the time I was ready for a serious relationship."

Andrew and Amber's story is packed with patience:

- patience in not manipulating a relationship for their own desires
- patience in waiting for a friendship to turn into something deeper
- patience in keeping their emotional and physical purity

The patience Andrew and Amber are living in their dating relationship comes from the foundation of their relationship in Christ. When we know we're chosen by Jesus, we can wait to be chosen by another!

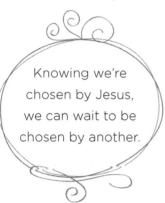

Knowing we're chosen by Jesus, we can wait to be chosen by another.

Ephesians 1:4–5 tells us, "For he chose us in him before the creation of the world to be holy and blameless in his sight. In love he predestined us to be adopted as his sons through Jesus Christ, in accordance with his pleasure and will."

God chose you before this planet was even created. How mind blowing! To think the God of the universe was thinking of us before any of this world was made! He chose you and me to be His.

He chose us not to make the cheerleading squad, not to get a degree or make it big, not even to find "the one" someday. All of those things might happen and would really be great if they did, but God has chosen you and me for something much bigger! He chose us to represent Him, showing the world the true definition of love.

That's why we're becoming magnetic: so we can show the world true love.

WHAT'S SO GREAT ABOUT THAT?

Maybe being God's display of love doesn't sound as exciting to you as traveling around the world, marrying a really hot guy, or driving a smoking car. What's so great about being His?

The girl inside you, the one who sometimes feels invisible, walks the halls alone, slips into her room after school, peers at her phone, and wonders, *Does anyone see me? Does anyone want me?* That girl is God's, chosen to be set apart. Not only did God make you to not be invisible, He also made you to stand out as His special one.

 Picture the most beautiful girl you know. What makes her so "perfect"? Her skin, shape, or style?

. . . .

. . . .

God has chosen you to stand out as an example of His perfection—with His perfect love shining through your life. His forgiving love washes away your sin, making you one gorgeous girl! Understanding how much He loves you will give you a confidence that cannot be shaken.

Picture a girl who feels chosen because she was...

- asked on a date.
- picked as homecoming queen.
- selected for her varsity team.

Can you see her face? She's beaming, eyes twinkling. Knowing she's chosen causes her to glow and be confident.

She's been set apart...

- to date the guy.
- to be the homecoming queen.
- to be a member of the team.

No wonder she's confident!

She is set apart for a purpose, to play a key role. She's...

- a girlfriend.
- a school representative.
- a team player.

The drawback? She can lose each one of these roles. Relationships break up, popularity fades, players get cut from the team.

But God...

God says He chose you, and He never changes His mind. He never cuts you from His team. He has a purpose and a plan for you! And it is a good plan. A very good plan! Sometimes, though, He will reveal that very good plan slowly. We must be patient as He matures us to handle His very good plan. Practicing patience now builds a foundation of strength and endurance for everything ahead.

PRACTICING PATIENCE WITH GOD

God's timetable is completely different from ours. Second Peter 3:8 gives us a glimpse into His big clock: "But do not forget this one thing, dear friends: With the Lord a day is like a thousand years, and a thousand years are like a day." How would you feel if God said He'd give you a boyfriend tomorrow? That could be a thousand years from now!

Seriously, our finite minds think in terms of minutes, hours, and days while God thinks long: months, years, eternity. The next verse tells us, "The Lord is not slow in keeping his promise, as some understand slowness. He is patient with you, not wanting anyone to perish, but everyone to come to repentance." We should be patient with Him because He has shown so much patience with us—and because we know He wants the best for us!

Earlier in this chapter we saw Andrew allude to what Paul says in Romans 8:27–28: "And he who searches our hearts knows the mind of the Spirit, because the Spirit intercedes for the saints in accordance with God's will. And we know that in all things God works for the good of those who love him, who have been called according to his purpose."

Even so, patience with God can be so hard, especially when we feel as though life is passing us by while we wait for God to do something. Lori shared, "I feel like I'm missing out. Like school is supposed to be great and amazing and it's not for me. Instead, it's a struggle. I know I'm going to do great in life, but right now I feel I'm just trying to get through."

Do you find it hard to believe God is working for your best and His? If so, why?

. . . .

. . . .

. . . .

. . . .

. . . .

So often, eager for those experiences announcing our arrival—first boyfriend, first kiss, first job, first apartment—we become impatient. We push our way, making things happen when we want them. The result: we end up with what we really don't want.

By contrast, when we understand and accept deep in our hearts God is in control, we can rest. He removes anxiety. Listen to David's testimony of change that came as he waited patiently for God:

> I waited patiently for the LORD; he turned to me and heard my cry. He lifted me out of the slimy pit, out of the mud and mire; he set my feet on a rock and gave me a firm place to stand. He put a new song in my mouth, a hymn of praise to our God. Many will see and fear and put their trust in the LORD. (Psalm 40:1–3)

You know how you feel when you desperately want something to happen but it isn't? You might not describe the experience as being stuck in a slimy pit of mud and mire, but it's definitely the pits.

I remember all too clearly being at school and far from home. So very alone, I wanted God to do something, bring someone! With the power of the Holy Spirit and with faith that God had my best at heart, I trusted Him. I made the hard decision to not work to get my way, but to rest in God's love for me. To run to Him instead of running for a guy. That time spent investing in my relationship with Jesus built a foundation of true love in my life so when the godly guy did come along, I was ready! I knew Greg was terrific, amazing, exactly what I wanted, but I also knew he didn't have what it took to completely fill a heart as empty as mine. Only Jesus could do that, and He already was!

> We push our way when we should have waited—and get what we really don't want.

Looking back, I'm so glad I trusted and waited on God. If I had dated Greg when I wanted to, when I was too young and immature to handle true love, he probably wouldn't have asked me to marry him many years later!

When you put the All-Powerful One in charge of your future, there is no reason to become impatient and force your way. Manipulation is dumb at best, disastrous at worst. When I force my way instead of waiting, a wreck is sure to follow. When I choose to be patient and calm, I can enjoy what God allows to come. Letting go of my expectations allows me to enjoy my life as it is.

Yes, being patient is beyond hard! We're afraid we might miss our only chance. We hear messages that build on that fear: "You've only got one shot at true love." "There's only one true love out there for you." When we see the guy we're sure is "the one," our heart can panic, prompting us to make something happen. Don't listen, friend. I know, I know—Disney movies taught us to just listen to our hearts. But here's the deal: Jeremiah 17:9 tells us, "The heart is deceitful above all things and beyond

cure. Who can understand it?" Our heart is
not always right! Our feelings and emotions
can steer us wrong, even lie to us. We have to
be patient and trust in the only thing that forever is true: our Jesus. Let the pressure fall on
Jesus, who can control the future, instead of on
you, who can't.

Wait. Don't
manipulate.

Can you see how knowing God is always on the lookout for your
best and His glory calms a girl down? Takes off the pressure to make life
happen?

The magnetic girl is patient with God. She knows He's working His
plan. She can wait, not manipulate.

PRACTICING PATIENCE WITH YOURSELF

A girl who knows she's loved by God is confident, the opposite of anxious
and awkward. She doesn't worry about having the right outfit or looking
just perfect. She doesn't struggle to be the best or create a perfect image.
She's not out to impress everyone. Why should she? She's already been
chosen! She's carefree. She can relax and have fun!

This is exactly what attracted Jake to Jamie: "The first thing I noticed about Jamie was her willingness to be spontaneous. The traits that
describe my girl are faithfulness, patience, kindness."

Contrast that description of God-infused confidence with the "I'm
better than others" attitude so many girls flaunt. Brandon observed,
"Confidence and arrogance are different. A lot of guys I know agree:
when girls flaunt it gets on our nerves. You can tell when a girl thinks she's
looking super good."

In my book *His Revolutionary Love,* I share, "When our need to feel
loved and valued is not filled by Jesus, that need becomes a force of

destruction in our lives. Satan knows what buttons to push to send us looking in the wrong places for our hearts to be filled. This need may show up in our lives in strange ways—masks for the real problem of an empty heart."[2]

You don't need to show off. That's for the insecure girl, the one who's impatient to be something she's not. Instead, you can radiate magnetic confidence, because you're moving...

- from unsure to sure.
- from insecure to secure.
- from unseen to seen.

A girl comfortable in her own skin is irresistible. Alex thinks so. Here's what he wanted to tell you: "Don't stray away from your true identity in Christ. Your activity branches from your identity. If you think that a guy could never love you, you won't allow yourself to be loved. If you see yourself as a child of God, you'll realize that you don't need approval from anyone else but Him. Realizing your true identity in Christ is so freeing. Don't allow people's opinions to dictate who you are. People will always have opinions; it doesn't mean they're right."

Practicing Patience with Others

Remember the opening story of the worn-out girl whose little sister stomped on her last nerve? That moment brought a choice: step into joy or smack it down. When we are tired and worn out, often we'll mess up and let impatience make the call. That day I was just plain rude, completely impatient. (Yeah, that story was a version of me!) Knowing how tired I was, I should have removed myself from the situation immediately. If that wasn't an option, I needed to choose patience and embrace another person's enthusiasm even when I was exhausted.

Proverbs 19:11 tells us, "A man's wisdom gives him patience; it is to his glory to overlook an offense."

When you read the word "glory," what comes to mind? I envision snowcapped mountains, gushing waterfalls, a coral-painted sunset—something so beautiful, I have to stop and soak in the sight.

The patient girl is so gorgeous others have to stop and soak in the sight of her. And this sight gives all the glory and attention to her Jesus!

Contrast this gorgeous girl with a short-tempered girl. No one wants to be around her. She is anything but charming! In fact, Isaiah listed "mean to other girls" as one trait that turns him off—and showing your annoyance is definitely mean.

Impatience is often the result of our thinking our way is better than anyone else's; we're prideful. Ecclesiastes 7:8–9 warns, "The end of a matter is better than its beginning, and patience is better than pride. Do not be quickly provoked in your spirit, for anger resides in the lap of fools."

I hate to admit it, but I've definitely been a fool a time or two. I could tell countless stories to prove it, beginning with my black eye when I was eight. Falling down concrete steps was my prize for being too impatient to wait for help. As I grew older, my pride and impatience caused much more painful consequences, which I would have traded gladly for a black eye!

When did your own impatience most recently get you a "black eye"?

. . . .
. . . .
. . . .
. . . .
. . . .

The patient girl is calm, easy going, even tempered, and long suffering. What isn't attractive about that? She's easy to be around because she finds a way to keep the mood cool and fun no matter what is happening. I want to hang out with her, to become like her.

Guys find confident patience appealing—and they notice when it's missing. When I interviewed Alex, he listed "super needy/high maintenance" in his top five things he finds unattractive!

Patience quietly says to others, "Because I trust God, the urge to rush or pressure guys will fade." Time and energy are no longer manipulative tools to use against a guy, but an opportunity to invest in him. Can you think of a girl who is patient like that, who doesn't pressure her guy to text ten times a day, carve out the weekend, or adjust his schedule for her?

Probably not.

That's just how rare this magnetic girl is. That's the girl you want to be!

Beautiful patience begins with humility. Pride believes she is right, others are wrong. The eye rolls and glares from across the table scream, "I'm better than you, more important than you, matter more than you." Nothing could be farther from the truth. Each and every person God creates is priceless.

Is someone in your life getting on your last nerve? The Bible has great advice: get humble. The key to patience with your frenemy is getting rid of pride, not getting rid of her!

"When a man's ways are pleasing to the LORD, he makes even his enemies live at peace with him" (Proverbs 16:7). What a promise! God's answer for drama relief: focus on pleasing Him, not ourselves.

Because we are God's, Paul urges us in Ephesians 4:2–3, "Be completely humble and gentle; be patient, bearing with one another in love.

Make every effort to keep the unity of the Spirit through the bond of peace."

We are wise when we choose to humble ourselves. Unfortunately, I have discovered that when I don't humble myself, God often gives me a helping hand with a humility adjustment.

Have you or a family member ever been to a chiropractor? You hop up on the table, and with a swift motion—*crack!*—the doctor pops your out-of-whack spine back into place.

Sometimes we need God to give us a swift *pop* to our pride and put us back in our place. When I attempted to write my first book, I was so excited! I just knew there was a publisher out there who couldn't wait to put me in print. Five years and nineteen rejections later, I was a humbler, gentler Lynn. What a painful and long experience! Not only did God deal with my pride, He worked on my patience too! Do I still struggle with pride? I do, but now I have my heart open to God's immediate correction! I don't want to go through that type of pain again!

We can choose to humble ourselves, letting God work through us, or we can choose to let God give us a humility adjustment! Both choices involve pain: the pain of choosing humility or the pain of God humbling us. The difference is one pain leads to growth and beauty while the other just leads to more pain.

When You Feel Like Freaking Out

Impatience often results when we're trying to control something or someone. Nobody likes to be controlled, so we end up in conflict when we insist things go our way. Patience restores peace—in ourselves and in our relationships.

Why did she start talking about peace? I hear you wondering. *I thought we had moved on to patience?* Like many of the captivating characteristics, peace and patience are connected. When you lack the peace that comes

Impatience outside reveals agitation inside.

with finding your confidence in Jesus, you'll have a hard time being patient. You'll feel anxious, driven to force things to go according to your plan instead of relaxing and trusting His plan. Impatience outside reveals agitation inside!

When your inner agitation tempts you to be impatient, you need to know how to live out of the fruit of the Spirit instead of living out of your feelings. Let me share with you a truth that has helped me out whenever I get sucked into trying to control my circumstances or other people.

Look up Psalm 37. Once you locate it, write PATIENCE next to it in the margin.

If we would memorize and obey the first three words, our impatience problem would no longer be a problem:

"Do not fret..."

The Hebrew root translated here as "fret" describes that churning we feel when we're impatient: angry, aroused, burning with anger. You might call it feeling anxious, annoyed, maybe even worried. All those things certainly drive my impatience at times!

Highlight or underline those three words "Do not fret" in your Bible. As we learn to depend on God, we're going to have to give our heart this command a time or two...or two hundred.

Now, start at the beginning of Psalm 37, then read this chapter out loud until you reach verse 6. I know. Reading out loud feels so weird! But it's a great way to really engage with the words and let them sink into your brain.

Do not fret because of evil men or be envious of those who do wrong; for like the grass they will soon wither, like green plants they will soon die away. Trust in the LORD and do good; dwell in the land and enjoy safe pasture. Delight yourself in the LORD and he will give you the desires of your heart. Commit your way to the LORD; trust in him and he will do this: He will make your righteousness shine like the dawn, the justice of your cause like the noonday sun.

David continues in this chapter to give us solid advice on what to do when our emotions run hot and our patience runs thin:

Be still before the LORD and wait patiently for him; do not fret when men succeed in their ways.... Refrain from anger...; do not fret—it leads only to evil. For evil men will be cut off, but those who hope in the LORD will inherit the land. (verses 7–9)

There's that command again: "Do not fret." In other words, don't freak out.

How many times does David say "do not fret" in these nine verses?

. . . .

. . . .

. . . .

. . . .

. . . .

. . . .

Sounds like we have to get this thing called impatience under control if we are going to enjoy God's best for us.

When you feel impatience stirring up your heart, stop a moment and ask yourself:

- *Am I fretting?* Say out loud, "Wait! Let God orchestrate!"
- *Am I being prideful?* Say out loud, "Choose humility; trust God."
- *Am I feeling agitated?* Say out loud, "Patience brings peace."

Keep Psalm 37:7 nearby. Write it in your phone notes and in bold Sharpie in your agenda: "Be still before the LORD and wait patiently for him; do not fret when men succeed in their ways, when they carry out their wicked schemes."

You know how good it feels to take a long, warm shower when you're completely worn out? When you find impatience taking you to the brink of your sanity, soak your mind in Psalm 37 and let it deliver patience to your worn-out heart.

ℰℰℰℰℰℰℰ

It won't be easy to choose patience and leave your life in God's hands. Every day you'll be tempted to seize control and take charge, to let other people know when they're stomping on your nerves, to pursue the attention of that guy you really want to notice you.

There are no shortcuts to becoming a magnetic girl. To follow Jesus takes discipline, denying yourself and living out patience. But I promise you, it will be totally worth it when you choose to let Him fulfill His perfect desires in your life.

Let's pray and ask the Holy Spirit to do in us what only He can do.

Jesus, I didn't realize how impatient I really am. Often I cut others down, feeling justified because they annoy me. Help me to worry less about others' actions and more about my own. I pledge to remove the word "annoying" from my vocabulary today. I choose to live out Your calming instruction: do not fret. I know You are continually at work in my life for my good. I choose to be patient with You as You are perfectly patient with me! I will wait and let You orchestrate! Amen.

No Need to Be Mean About It

Cultivating Kindness

When I think of kindness, one young woman in particular comes to mind. She's not exactly what you'd call outspoken. In fact, shy is a better description. In our small group of girls, Alexandra is the one I have to draw out a bit, asking questions to hear what's on her mind. But under Alexandra's quiet exterior lies a strength few girls will ever know.

The summer before her sophomore year, Alexandra received terrifying news: she needed major surgery to correct scoliosis. An incision would be made from her neck to her tailbone so the surgeon could insert two rods with twenty-one screws in her spine and correct the fifty-eight-degree curve in her back.

Was she scared? You bet! But I watched that summer as she prepared her heart and mind for the biggest fight she'd faced so far. In her quiet way, her words revealed a girl who expected God to show up.

And He did. Just days after invasive surgery, Alexandra walked the halls of that hospital. In two short weeks, she was sitting through geometry.[3]

Throughout this physical challenge and the months of healing that followed, Alexandra demonstrated powerful magnetic traits. Perhaps most surprisingly, she has allowed trauma to create softness in her heart.

Alexandra consistently demonstrates kindness as a member of Curvy Girls, a group that supports those facing the same scoliosis treatment she endured. She visits other patients before or after surgery, bringing gifts and encouragement.

Kindness spills over into other areas of her life too. Last Christmas, our small group created gift boxes for Operation Christmas Child. We delivered those boxes to the Samaritan's Purse warehouse, where we packed boxes for underprivileged children around the world. Beaming, Alexandra used her time and energy to bring joy to children she would never meet—at least not on this planet. "I would love to do this every day!" she told me. In Alexandra I see beautiful proof: those who give kindness receive happiness!

It Pays to Be Kind

Kindness is all about putting someone else's needs and desires above our own. It's the generosity that gives your little brother the last cookie, sits down at lunch with the girl who's all alone, and chooses to see the best in others rather than focus on their flaws. Jeremiah 9:23–24 tells us,

> Let not the wise man boast of his wisdom or the strong man boast of his strength or the rich man boast of his riches, but let him who boasts boast about this: that he understands and knows me, that I am the Lord, who exercises kindness, justice and righteousness on earth, for in these I delight.

Kindness is not just a suggestion from God, a trait to make us attractive. It is a command to us from our Creator. Micah 6:8 says, "He has showed you, O man, what is good; and what does the LORD require of you but to do justice, and to love kindness, and to walk humbly with your God?" (RSV).

In the verses before this passage, the Lord reminded His people, the Israelites, of all the kindness He had shown to them, including redeeming them from slavery and sending them a leader in Moses. So He asked how they would show their thanks to Him—and then He told them exactly how He wanted them to worship Him: act justly, be kind, and walk humbly with God.

When I show kindness to another person, I am worshiping God, showing Him how much I love Him. Yet it's not just for God's benefit or even for the person I am being kind to. Kindness comes with a reward for me.

In our experience, we know that if we plant tomato seeds in the ground, we get a tomato plant (provided we remembered to water the garden!). It's the principle of sowing and reaping. What's true in the physical world is also true in the spiritual life of a Jesus follower. What we plant in how we treat others comes back in our lives. Plant kindness, get kindness.

"Do not be deceived: God cannot be mocked. A man reaps what he sows. The one who sows to please his sinful nature, from that nature will reap destruction; the one who sows to please the Spirit, from the Spirit will reap eternal life" (Galatians 6:7–8).

It pays to be kind! Alexandra has experienced firsthand the benefit of being kind to others. The Lord has been kind to her, healed her back, and restored her to health. While she has some limitations, such as not being able to jump on a trampoline, you would never know looking at her that she has experienced major surgery.

To become the girls God wants us to be, we need to plant seeds of kindness in those around us, whether toward our best friend or the one who seems completely different. The Micah 6:8 command to be kind applies to our interactions with everyone, even our enemies.

Check out Proverbs 25:21–22: "If your enemy is hungry, give him food to eat; if he is thirsty, give him water to drink. In doing this, you will heap burning coals on his head, and the LORD will reward you."

When we give our "enemies" what they need—love and kindness—instead of what they deserve, God will reward us. As we invest kindness into the lives of others, God will make sure we receive kindness in return.

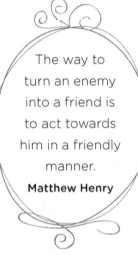

The way to turn an enemy into a friend is to act towards him in a friendly manner.

Matthew Henry

Unfortunately, this principle of reaping what we sow works the other way too. When we choose to pass along the story of the girl at school who gets around, we can know for sure unkindness in some form will come back to us.

In our culture, meanness has become the norm among girls and women today. The sarcastic comment, the sly insult, the silent treatment—all these and more have become commonplace as we vie for the power position in our relationships. But in the process, are we setting the stage for our own heartache?

Proverbs gives those of us living life God's way great advice: "The wise woman builds her house, but with her own hands the foolish one tears hers down" (14:1). The wise woman builds up her family, using kindness. An unwise woman is her own worst enemy, using unkindness to tear apart. The time to practice "building your home" is now! Girls don't suddenly become kind when they grow up. The kindness you practice today is the kindness that will mark your life tomorrow. Decisions you're making now and the habits you're establishing shape the kind of woman, the kind of friend, the kind of wife you will be one day.

 The choices you make today shape the woman you'll be tomorrow. Who are you becoming?

. . . .
. . . .
. . . .
. . . .
. . . .

Work toward the future you want.

The Kind Girl Is the Kind He Wants

Guys most definitely notice how we treat others. As we saw in the chapter on patience, Isaiah listed "mean to those around her" as one of his no-go qualities. By contrast, Caleb said, "Kindness is a big characteristic I look for. If a girl is really kind and always looking to do good, that's an awesome characteristic!"

The kind girl stands out in a good way. She's actively making a difference in her world. She's all about giving, not getting. And what guy wouldn't appreciate that? It's all part of the total package a godly guy will be looking for in the woman he trusts with his heart.

Grab your Bible and let's check out Proverbs 31 together. This unique passage is essentially a mother's letter to her son, the king, telling him exactly what he should look for in a woman. She's not describing a specific

Are You Quick to Be Kind?

How about taking a quick quiz to see how you're doing with the trait of kindness? Add up your score on this quiz and compare it to the scale at the end.

A) Your little sister is going to a party and says she has nothing to wear. You...

  1. ignore her and hope she doesn't ask to borrow anything.
  2. pick out your least favorite shirt and ask if she wants to wear it.
  3. invite her to come to your closet and see if she can find something she'd like to wear.

B) You sit next to a girl in choir who is tone deaf. You...

  1. complain to your friends how bad it is.
  2. pretend it isn't happening.
  3. give her a reassuring smile during class.

C) Your friend just got dumped by her boyfriend. You...

  1. make plans so you don't have to hear about it.

2. listen for a while, then change
the subject.

3. do your best to comfort her.

D) Your single friend is over when your boyfriend
shows up for your date. You...

1. say "See you later" as you
and your guy head down the
driveway.

2. let her know you'll catch up
with her later in the night.

3. invite her to hang out with
the two of you for a little
while.

How did you do? If you got...

10–12 points: You are well on your way to
becoming the girl He wants!

7–9 points: Sometimes you're choosing kindness, but ask the Holy Spirit to help you to
become more consistent.

4–6 points: Looks like kindness needs to
become a focus area for you as you seek
the Holy Spirit's help.

Be sure to record your score in the back of
the book, so you can identify your strengths as
well as the areas where you need to seek God's
help.

woman she knows, but instead is listing for King Lemuel the qualities and characteristics he should look for in a girl to marry.

She starts out with a couple of warnings:

- Don't waste your energy on the type of girl who will ruin you.
- Don't drink wine and crave beer; you'll make bad choices.

Then Mom gets into her full-blown description of the right girl, the magnetic girl, starting in verse 10: "A wife of noble character who can find? She is worth far more than rubies."

"Noble character." Sounds so royal. King Lemuel's mom says, "Son, if you find this girl, you'll be one rich man. But who can find her?" She admits that the woman who possesses these captivating characteristics is rare. "But you can find her," she assures him. "And make sure you do! She is priceless!"

Mama Lemuel goes on to describe how kindness shows up in this rare girl's life:

Her husband has full confidence in her and lacks nothing of value. She brings him good, not harm, all the days of her life. She selects wool and flax and works with eager hands. She is like the merchant ships, bringing her food from afar. She gets up while it is still dark; she provides food for her family and portions for her servant girls. (verses 11–15)

No wonder the Bible says, "Her husband has full confidence in her." This woman shows kindness in the way she treats him, her family, and those who serve her!

The poor also receive her kindness: "She opens her arms to the poor and extends her hands to the needy" (verse 20). She's not wrapped up in herself. She is motivated to give, not get ahead. I'm guessing she has found that giving kindness brings her happiness just like Alexandra!

Through her description, King Lemuel's mom tells him, "Look for the girl who's looking out for others." Her day isn't consumed with shopping for the latest designer bag, sweating out her workout, and getting her nails done. Although these things may have a place in her life, they aren't her life. Her time is spent investing in others, displaying kindness through caring.

Those who respect you the most should be the ones who know you the best.
Andy Stanley

What kind of reward goes to a woman who chooses serving others instead of serving herself? Her reward comes from those who receive her kindness: "Her children arise and call her blessed; her husband also, and he praises her" (verse 28). Those who see her day in and day out value her character and can say only good about her!

Our author finishes the chapter with this powerful reminder: " 'Many women do noble things, but you surpass them all.' Charm is deceptive, and beauty is fleeting; but a woman who fears the LORD is to be praised" (verses 29–30).

Twenty years from now, if you become a wife and mom, how would you want your husband and children to describe you?

. . . .
. . . .
. . . .
. . . .
. . . .

True respect is the reward of a life characterized by kindness. That's a reward I want; don't you?

DEATH TO INNER UGLINESS

So how do we become this amazing Proverbs 31 girl, unselfish and kind?

When choosing others over myself, my brain argues, *Who's going to look out for me?* Ugly, I know. Discouraging too. But as we practice kindness and putting others first, kindness can become our natural response. As we grow more and more dependent on God, we see He's the One looking out for us, and there couldn't be anyone better!

Remember the words of our key passage: "The fruit of the Spirit is love, joy, peace, patience, *kindness,* goodness, faithfulness" (Galatians 5:22, emphasis added).

The truth we need to keep in the forefront of our minds is that this passage describes the fruit of the Spirit. Not the fruit of determination. Not the fruit of self-effort. Certainly not the fruit of Lynn. The fruit of Lynn is self-centered, prideful, egotistical, and narcissistic. Not exactly beautiful! It is called the fruit of the Spirit because it takes God Himself living His life through me for these qualities to be evident in my life. That fruit comes only when I am broken away from the *me* I described, when I no longer live for me, but He lives out of me. I need His power for this transformation to happen!

Galatians 2:20 tells us, "I have been crucified with Christ and I no longer live, but Christ lives in me. The life I live in the body, I live by faith in the Son of God, who loved me and gave himself for me."

When I made the decision to follow Jesus, there was a death involved: mine. Following Jesus means we die to the ugly side of ourselves so that the life of Christ can live in us.

The magnetic girl has learned she's better off dead—dead to herself. Only then can she be fully alive to Jesus living in and through her.

THE ULTIMATE MEASURE OF KINDNESS

Jesus takes kindness to the level of an extreme sport, compelling us to stretch muscles we didn't know we had. As He told His followers, "If you love those who love you, what credit is that to you? For even 'sinners' love those who love them" (Luke 6:32).

Jesus lived out kindness in ways that sometimes shocked the people around Him. In John 8, we find Him teaching in the temple. The religious people brought to Jesus a woman they caught having sex with someone who wasn't her husband. They wanted Jesus to make her pay for her awful sin. The law demanded stoning to death the one caught in adultery. What Jesus did next stunned the religious people—the woman too, I'm sure!

Jesus simply bent over and wrote something in the ground with His finger. Then He straightened up, and to those who thought they were so much better than this "sinner," He simply said, "If any one of you is without sin, let him be the first to throw a stone at her" (verse 7). Convicted, the judgmental ones walked away one at a time, until only Jesus was left.

Instead of giving the adulterous woman what she deserved, Jesus gave her kindness. Though she didn't "deserve" to have someone stand up for her, He did it anyway.

Jesus is the perfect model of perfect kindness, perfect love. He extends that same perfect kindness to you and me. Titus 3:4–5 reminds us, "When the kindness and love of God our Savior appeared, he saved us, not because of righteous things we had done, but because of his mercy."

In what ways has Jesus been kind to you?

. . . .

. . . .

. . . .

. . . .

. . . .

Our God has shown us the ultimate act of kindness by forgiving us. It's time for us to take the kindness we have been shown, then turn around and share it with the one who doesn't deserve it and with those who cannot repay.

When we soak each day in His kindness, we can be like Jesus, giving "undeserved" kindness to others. Spending time reading the Gospels of the New Testament is just one way we can immerse our hearts. Seeing how Jesus was kind to others gives us a clear model to follow in our own lives. We can also flood our hearts with worship music and spend time talking to Him in prayer. As we do, He will pour into us the power to be kind to the bully in the hall, the mean girl on social media, or the unreasonable parent.

CALLED INTO KINDNESS

Meet my friend Kelsey, who understands exactly what it means to be kind and share God's kindness. "I love to be comfortable," Kelsey told me. "I grew up comfortable. Jesus was the central figure of our Christian family. I graduated from a Christian high school and college. I enjoyed every bit of my comfortable life when God decided I needed some 'pulling out of comfort.'

"I think as Christians, when we get comfortable, God gets busy. We weren't created to be 'safe' and love Jesus at the same time. When we say yes to God, we step into the greatest adventure of all. But to me, adventure means scary. I'm not adventurous. I even get nervous talking about my faith to my friends. *What will they think about me? Will they see me as a freak? Who am I to tell them to change their lives?* I did the next best thing: lived my life and prayed silently for them to change theirs. Sure, I knew the best life is with Jesus, but I never felt like I could stand up, step out, and tell others about Him."

Does Kelsey's description of her silent witness sound familiar? As much as we want our friends to know God the way we do, sometimes we get so caught up in worries about sounding weird that we resist sharing His love. But as Kelsey discovered, God wants so much more for us and from us.

She continued her story: "While sitting in church, I felt God whisper three little words to me that changed my life: *Love My daughters.*

"I thought that sounded pretty simple: start another Bible study, increase prayers for family and friends, fund a bake sale. Simple. Easy. Comfortable. Fortunately for me, He meant so much more."

Kelsey soon realized that when God said, *Love My daughters,* He meant His daughters in the sex industry. He meant girls and women caught in stripping, prostitution, and pornography.

"I flipped out!" she told me of her response to God's urging. "*You want me to go where? You want me to love who?* I was a wreck. I couldn't do that. That wasn't what Christians did. It wasn't easy, simple, or comfortable, which is exactly why it was God's plan."

The good news about being called by God to step out of your comfort zone is that He will pave the way for you to follow where He leads.

"Shortly after this ginormous 'God moment,'" Kelsey said, "I had a unique opportunity to intern with a transitional home for women coming out of the sex industry, a refuge and healing place for ladies who simply need Jesus and rest from the lifestyle they've lived. One of my responsibilities was helping to organize the ministry's spring gala.

"Now, I love parties, so the gala was right up my alley! Months of planning led up to a night where we would gather the most influential people in our area for an unforgettable evening of raising awareness and helping people in our community see the impact of the sex industry.

If you're not out of your comfort zone, you aren't doing something right.

Steven Furtick

"God pulled off every detail of this elaborate evening," Kelsey declared. "Makeup artists, salon stylists, restaurants—the list of those who donated their services went on and on. Greatest of all, seventy formal dresses were donated to our girls for the night! A few weeks before the gala, we had a party at my house so the girls could pick out their dress. The comments were amazing: 'I've never felt so beautiful!' 'I haven't worn a dress since I was little!' 'I feel like Cinderella!'"

Can't you just picture those women twirling and spinning, caught up in the joy of feeling beautiful and beloved?

Kelsey's own excitement came through as she described the big event: "God had in mind from the beginning to show His kindness! The night of the gala, I saw these precious women realize for the first time in a long time they were valued, loved, and adored for who they were, not what they could do. Two of the women sang songs of praise while another graduate told her story. Jesus was in the room that night, looking each woman full in the face and telling her, 'I love you for you. You are beautiful. You are cherished. You are Mine.' That night I stood in awe of Jesus. I witnessed a miracle! What an honor and a privilege to love God's girls as He would. We were like sisters long separated but brought close through God's perfect plan.

"At the end of the night we whispered, 'Wow, God.' Not because of the money raised, dinner served, or beautiful people who attended. Instead we celebrated the new women these girls were because of Jesus. Every guest saw how these precious lives had been changed."

In summarizing her experience of stepping out into the unknown to share God's kindness, Kelsey said she felt overwhelmed and humbled by all she'd witnessed during the past year. "Jesus wanted me to be uncomfortable so I could find my comfort in Him. He wanted me to feel nervous so I would turn to Him for my peace. He wanted me to step outside of my own little boundaries so I could truly experience the life He has always planned for me.

"Today, I'm like a new person. Kelsey: lover of Jesus and friend of sex workers. And you know the best part? I'm living outside of my comfort zone every single day, showing His kindness."

KINDNESS: COSTS SO LITTLE, GIVES SO MUCH

Kelsey's story offers the perfect example of a magnetic girl—one whose love for Jesus propels her to show kindness to people who can't do anything to repay her.

Of course, your opportunities to demonstrate kindness will look different from hers. But every day, almost every hour, each of us has occasion to give away kindness—to our family members, to our friends, to the clerk at the grocery store checkout, to everyone who crosses our path. Kindness isn't about just doing the big stuff; it's about everyday, ordinary moments in which we deliberately choose to honor others above ourselves.

When we make kindness the habit of our lives, when we consciously choose to set aside our wants and look for ways to encourage and uplift other people, the irresistible light of Jesus shines through us, drawing others to Him.

Just consider how Andrew describes the kindness he sees his girl-friend, Amber, show to others: "Amber assumes the best in people. This is good for me; kindness doesn't always come easy to me. She is constantly putting my needs ahead of her own! Simple kindnesses like doing the dishes, cleaning my car, or surprising me with a milkshake really mean the most. I'm encouraged to do kind acts for her, which improves and strengthens our relationship.

"I'll never forget one day," he continued, "when I truly saw Jesus's kindness in Amber. We went to volunteer at a nursing home. She sort of dragged me along, and I ended up being the only boy. While playing bingo, Amber assisted an elderly lady who was very hard of hearing. As I read the bingo ball, Amber enthusiastically shouted again each call. It was hilarious. Everyone at her table was having the time of their lives. These simple acts truly make the difference in a relationship centered on Jesus Christ."

Can't you just picture Amber loudly echoing Andrew's every call? Rather than being irritated by the limitations of the older woman, Amber allowed the kindness of Jesus to spill over to those around her. As a result, everyone had a great time!

That's the beauty of kindness: it costs us so little yet everyone, including us, gains so much in return!

Jesus, kindness does not come naturally for me. Being selfish and self-centered does. As I learn more about You, empower me to make choices every day to die to that selfish girl and become one magnetic woman! Amen.

Beauty in a Pure Heart

Finding Strength in Goodness

What a turnaround! When I first met Anne and she joined our small group, she knew of Jesus but didn't really know Jesus. As her life changed and goodness began to define Anne's choices, her fresh passion brought new life to our small group.

"Giving my life to Jesus Christ was one of the hardest things I have ever done, but the best decision I've ever made," Anne wrote me. "I didn't think I could change just by believing or trusting in Someone greater than anything on this earth. Boy, was I wrong! God saved me; He brought me out of the darkness and into the light."

Anne described a bit of that darkness: "Known as not the best person to hang around, I got into trouble frequently. Extremely self-conscious, being accepted was most important to me. My friendships were valuable based on whether or not they benefited me or made me feel good. Passive-aggressive and catty, I wasn't nice; I often talked behind people's backs and got jealous easily. Since I hated my body—actually I hated myself—this made it easier for me to hate other people."

Can you relate to the misery of not liking who you are but not knowing how to change? Anne described how she is finding the beautiful she longs to become: "A couple of months ago, I starting praying, asking God to soften my heart and help me be a good person! That's when I began to be the new me. I gave my everything to the Lord, and I really began to change.

"Every day I pray to God to help me to show the fruit of the Spirit, and every day I am becoming a better person than the one I was just a few months ago. Even my family and friends have noticed! Since the day I surrendered my life to Jesus, I am happy with who I am! In fact, I love myself!"

Isn't that amazing? Seeing this change in Anne is really exciting. But that doesn't mean she now always finds it easy to choose right.

"Being God's girl means I have to say no to a lot of things," she told me. "Yes, it does make me seem like a goody two-shoes, but I know saying no to those things is part of God's path for me. He has a wonderful future for me, and sometimes to get that future you have to stand alone with your beliefs. I know, though, that I am never really alone. The Lord will never abandon me; He will always be with me. I have to stand strong with my faith.

"One of my favorite verses is Psalm 16:8: 'I have set the LORD always before me. Because he is at my right hand, I will not be shaken.' "

If you took a survey at your school asking people to define *goodness* or to explain what makes something good, I'm sure you'd get a bunch of different answers. That's because most people think *good* means "what feels right" or "what benefits me." What often fuels people's choices is what they think is good *for them*.

How would you define *goodness*?

. . . .
. . . .
. . . .
. . . .
. . . .
. . . .

As Christ followers, we find in the Bible our true standard of goodness: "Anyone, then, who knows the good he ought to do and doesn't do it, sins" (James 4:17).

Author and pastor Mark Batterson observed, "Goodness is not the absence of badness. You can do nothing wrong and still do nothing right. Those who simply run away from sin are half-Christians. Our calling is much higher than simply running away from what's wrong."[4]

Goodness is not found just by avoiding bad; we need to plan for and do good!

Goodness is demonstrated when we choose behavior pleasing to God, such as being kind and avoiding evil. Justice, righteousness, holiness, purity, gentleness, and kindness are just a few traits demonstrating goodness.

Every day in all our relationships we have opportunities to show goodness, and this begins when we do something that is solely for the benefit of others.

Too often, the motivation behind our choices is me: *What's in it for me? Does this person make me feel good? Is he there for me when I need him? Does he make me look good?* We put ourselves in the spotlight, not looking out for others' good.

Goodness calls us to make it about *we* instead of *me*! When we do

Are You Good and Ready to Choose Goodness?

Let's see whether goodness is a strength or a weakness in your life. Add up your score on this quiz and compare it to the scale at the end.

A) You find out the night before the deadline that you've done your English project completely wrong. You...

 1. quickly copy your sister's project from two years ago.
 2. call in sick, buying yourself another day.
 3. stay up all night to redo it right.

B) You and your boyfriend are really struggling to be pure in your physical relationship. You...

 1. give in. You're planning on getting married someday anyway.
 2. cross some lines but don't go all the way.
 3. decide never to be together alone in the dark.

C) A few girls at your lunch table constantly make fun of other girls' outfits. You...

1. agree—some girls have no sense of style.
2. keep quiet, since they're just going to do it anyway.
3. ask them to stop.

D) An organization for homeless kids needs tutors. You...

1. decide you're too busy. You have your own grades to worry about.
2. consider fitting it in your senior year.
3. volunteer, bringing your friends along.

How did you do?

10–12 points: You get it! The captivating characteristic of goodness is pouring out of you!

7–9 points: Sometimes you choose God's way, other times your own.

4–6 points: You can shine goodness, but you need to start depending on God!

Be sure to record your score in the back of the book, so you can identify your strengths as well as the areas where you need to seek God's help.

something for someone strictly for his or her good, without hidden motives to make us happy, we show a love that is mature and unselfish.

"But wait!" you say. "No one else is doing this, looking out for other people first. Who's going to look out for me?" What a nasty trap, comparing ourselves to others. Next to other people, we might look pretty great! But our measuring stick isn't based on those around us. Our measurement for good is God Himself. Keeping our eyes on Him, not the girls around us, helps us become more like Jesus.

Anne emphasized that every day she needs the Lord to help her shine the fruit of the Spirit. Becoming the girl God wants her to be requires her to depend on Him. Becoming good is not simply trying harder. When we try harder, we'll eventually fail. Selfishness naturally slithers through our thoughts and actions. As the psalmist said, "There is no one who does good, not even one" (Psalm 14:3). For goodness to bloom in our lives, it has to be planted and tended by God in our hearts.

NOT EVEN A HINT OF IMPURITY

Ephesians 5:3–4 sets our standard for goodness: "But among you there must not be *even a hint* of sexual immorality, or of *any kind* of impurity, or of greed, because these are improper for God's holy people. Nor should there be obscenity, foolish talk or coarse joking, which are out of place, but rather thanksgiving" (emphasis added).

Maybe, like me, you felt a pang in your heart as you read these verses, especially that phrase "there must not be even a hint." God isn't leaving *any* room in our heart or actions for what is inappropriate. This includes what we might define as "big sins," such as sex outside of marriage, and those we think of as "little." Foolish talking and coarse joking are just as wrong for those who are His.

You might have wondered, *Why so strict? What's wrong with a little fun? God needs to lighten up.* As I started reading the Bible, I discovered God definitely isn't against fun and celebrating. The Old Testament is full of times when God tells His people to celebrate. But God knows if we let even a little bit of inappropriate joking into our lives, we quickly grow used to it. What was crude quickly becomes cool. From there, it's a slippery slope to a contaminated heart and perverted actions.

When I was the new girl in my high school, I faced a lot of choices when it came to fitting in. When I was invited to parties or asked out by guys who weren't Christ followers, my answer was always the same: no. Afraid I'd make an unwise choice, I decided the best way was avoiding it all. Don't go to parties, don't date guys I don't know, don't lie to sneak out. Soon, they just quit inviting me.

At first, I was glad; at least I no longer had to wrestle over the right decision. Finding a couple of girls who had similar values, girls who also loved Jesus, made a big difference. To help us get through this road loaded with temptations, each day we would write out verses on index cards for each other. In between classes, we'd swap cards. God's Word was literally filling my heart all day long!

But as time passed, I didn't keep fueling my heart with Jesus. I grew tired of being good and started feeling left out. One Friday, my friend and I were invited to a party at a boy's house. She said, "Let's go!" I wasn't so sure. I'd heard rumors his parents wouldn't be home. Since my friend loved Jesus and was okay with going, I pushed aside my conscience and joined her.

When I pulled up to the house, the street was loaded with cars. *Do the neighbors know his parents are out of town? What do they think is going on?* Images of police swarming in flashed through my mind. Each step to the house echoed in my pounding heart.

Slipping in the back door, I hit wall-to-wall people. Kids were everywhere, in every room, in every corner—many people I knew, many I didn't. And then, I spotted it. The counter covered with alcohol.

My mind whirled with questions: *Should I go or should I stay? If I go, what will they think of me? I like hanging out with them at school; they're so nice! This is my chance to show I'm not too good to hang out with them. I can handle this. But these people know I love Jesus. If I stay, what will they think of me? What will they think of Him?*

My heart knew the answer. "I'm leaving," I told my friend.

"Wait," she protested. "We just got here!"

I had already made up my mind to do the wise thing—leave. Now.

Good girls don't just go along—they stand strong.

Even if it meant I left alone. Since my friend had driven herself, I left her with the decision of what was wise for her. With each step toward my car, my heart lifted, my stomach calmed. *Thank You, Jesus. I needed You and You helped me.*

Maybe you've been in a similar situation. Maybe you haven't. Either way, I'm certain you've faced an opportunity to choose goodness—right living—when doing so meant your friends might feel awkward, possibly even angry. Here's the truth for those who want to follow Jesus: good girls don't just go along—they stand strong.

When I agreed to go to that party, my heart was heading away from God in order to justify what I wanted to do. I deliberately hardened myself to resist the thoughts telling me my choice would be wrong.

The girl who values goodness stands strong for what's right. She keeps a soft heart toward God so she can follow Him. She blends softness and strength. A soft heart is one God can mold to be more like Jesus's every day.

FEEDING YOUR SOUL ON GOODNESS

I so want you to become a girl who goes to the Bible for yourself so you can learn what God wants for you. This is why I include so much scripture in this book; His words are so much more powerful than mine!

So for this section, let's dig around a little bit in Ephesians 5. Got your Bible? We'll start in the middle of this chapter: "For you were once darkness, but now you are light in the Lord. Live as children of light (for the fruit of light consists in all goodness, righteousness and truth) and find out what pleases the Lord" (verses 8–10).

Remember when Anne said God "brought me out of the darkness and into the light"? Before we asked Jesus to forgive our sins and give us His new life, we were in darkness. If you walk into a room that is pitch black, you can't see anything. You'll probably bump into furniture, run into a wall, even hurt yourself!

Darkness in our spiritual lives is similar; because we can't see, we don't distinguish good from bad very well. In Ephesians 4:17–19, Paul explains this phenomenon, "With the Lord's authority I say this: Live no longer as the Gentiles do, for they are hopelessly confused. Their minds are full of darkness; they wander far from the life God gives because they have closed their minds and hardened their hearts against him. They have no sense of shame. They live for lustful pleasure and eagerly practice every kind of impurity" (NLT).

Those who live for themselves, in spiritual darkness, become numb to goodness. Sin seems normal. God's ways don't make sense. These people have been deceived, duped into thinking this cruddy lifestyle is great, a fun way to live. And they get pulled deeper and deeper into polluted living. Their souls are so starved for truth that what is gross, tainted, and nasty actually starts to look good. But living in darkness only brings loneliness and shame, trapping them in a cycle of searching for something to satisfy their empty hearts.

> Have you ever been caught in a dark situation, but you didn't see it clearly?

. . . .
. . . .
. . . .
. . . .
. . . .

Paul says those of us who have Jesus don't have to stumble around in the darkness, confused about what's good and what's not. We can walk in the light of "all goodness, righteousness and truth" (Ephesians 5:9). To walk in this light, we have to choose to feed our souls the goodness of God; otherwise we can easily get pulled back into the deception of darkness. Pulled into a cycle of sin.

Just look around; you'll see it's true. Some of the guys I interviewed see it too.

Andrew said, "I can truly say that finding a good Christian girl with godly morals and principles is a difficult struggle, even at a Christian university. Girls often talk the talk, but rarely walk the walk."

Adam echoed this opinion: "Yeah, it was hard to find someone; most girls don't carry godly attributes. Many are superficial; they see dating as a status symbol. They'll wear hardly anything just to make some guy look at them. You don't have to be a nun, but present yourself in a way that you would want to once you do have a husband. It's a reflection of your faithfulness to your man and God."

Do you feel a little bit embarrassed on behalf of girls everywhere after reading these guys' accounts? I do! Moms used to have to teach their sons not to make advances on girls. Now moms have to teach their sons to resist advances from girls!

We can reverse this trend by becoming good, living in the light of Jesus. We can bring back classy! As we mirror His goodness, our lives will reflect a rare beauty!

A PURIFIED MIND

This beauty starts as we ask Jesus to clean out of us all that blurs or mars His reflection. Remember when we talked about training the brain? It's the same process for becoming good. Ephesians 4:23 tells us to "be made new in the attitude of your minds." It all begins with cleaning our thinking.

Think about that dirty laundry piling up in your hamper (or on your floor). If your clothes are going to get clean, they have to go through the washing machine. If you are going to get clean, you've got to take a spin in the washing machine of God's presence. The spotless spin—the place where He cleanses our hearts and minds, purifying us of anything not good—takes place as we spend more and more time with Him. Here's how David describes the spotless spin in Psalm 24:3–6:

> Who may ascend the hill of the LORD? Who may stand in his
> holy place? He who has clean hands and a pure heart, who does
> not lift up his soul to an idol or swear by what is false. He will
> receive blessing from the LORD and vindication from God his
> Savior. Such is the generation of those who seek him, who seek
> your face, O God of Jacob.

The more we experience God's presence, the purer our hearts become. That's how the polluted pattern of sin is broken—seeking God's face! Will you be one of the precious few pursuing Him with all of your heart, wanting more than anything to be good like Him?

Have you asked Jesus to forgive you for your sins and give you His new life? If so, write out what that experience has looked like. If not, you can ask Him for this new life right now!

. . . .
. . . .
. . . .
. . . .
. . . .

What's a girl to do if her heart is hard? What if her mind resists God's words, maybe even gets aggravated and a little mad about His ways? You can be sure if you reach out to Him, He is reaching out to you. He promises,

> I will sprinkle clean water on you, and you will be clean; I will cleanse you from all your impurities and from all your idols. I will give you a new heart and put a new spirit in you; I will remove from you your heart of stone and give you a heart of flesh. And I will put my Spirit in you and move you to follow my decrees and be careful to keep my laws. (Ezekiel 36:25–27)

I know this is true from personal experience. Even though I was making mostly good decisions as a young adult, my heart was growing away from God instead of toward Him, becoming hard. On the outside, my actions looked good, but I was tired of being different and going against the crowd. One wise decision I made during this time was to go to Bible school. There, as I surrendered the heart I had and told God I wanted all of Him and He could have all of me, my heart became soft once again. That surrender came as a result of many hours doing what I didn't necessarily feel like doing: listening to teaching from God's Word and additional hours reading God's Word on my own.

As a result, not only did my actions change to being good for me and for God, I also began to practice being good to others. Being good happens as we saturate our minds with God's Word and then do what it says. His goodness fills our hearts and flows out to others.

WHAT'S INSIDE COMES OUT

Jesus explained the connection between having His goodness in our hearts and demonstrating goodness in our lives: "For out of the overflow of the heart the mouth speaks. The good man brings good things out of the good stored up in him, and the evil man brings evil things out of the evil stored up in him" (Matthew 12:34–35). It's simple: what we pour in pours out!

All too often goodness is not what pours out of our mouths. Our tongues are hard to control; they seem to have a mind of their own!

What we pour in pours out!

Our minds are still in the process of being changed by God's Word, so at times, we still have thoughts that are anything but good! And when we let those ugly thoughts fly out of our mouths, we end up cutting down others or being rude. Failing to use a filter brings pain to others and damages our relationships.

The Holy Spirit wants to interrupt this pattern. If you ask, He will help you stop and think about your thoughts *before* they become your words. God's Word teaches us how to use our mouths for good:

Do not let any unwholesome talk come out of your mouths,
but only what is helpful for building others up according to
their needs, that it may benefit those who listen.… Get rid
of all bitterness, rage and anger, brawling and slander, along
with every form of malice. Be kind and compassionate to one
another, forgiving each other, just as in Christ God forgave
you. (Ephesians 4:29, 31–32)

Can you imagine how gorgeous we can become when the only
words we speak are words for good? Seem impossible? Not when God is
helping us!

Putting boundaries on your words might require you to even become
known as "the quiet girl" for a time. Sound drastic? When our mouths
are taking us in the wrong direction, we need drastic measures to get on
the right path.

WHEN GOODNESS GOES WRONG

In our pursuit of goodness, we need to beware of the pitfall of becoming
Pharisees. The Pharisees were these religious guys in the Bible who were
so worried about looking good they missed being loving. Several times,
they even criticized Jesus for healing on the Sabbath, as if the rules were
more important than caring for those in need.

Quick to judge, I've sometimes played the Pharisee, wondering what
everyone else's problem is—why can't they just obey God?

To avoid pride and looking down on others who don't get everything
exactly right, the girl partnering with God needs the fruit of both goodness and kindness. A girl focused solely on goodness risks becoming
proud, self-righteous, focused on how good she looks compared to others.
So busy judging, she misses why people act the way they do, not seeing

their hurts or the love they need. On the other hand, the girl giving all her attention to kindness might be lackadaisical about goodness, willing to overlook what shouldn't be.

Combining kindness and goodness brings God's best. When our lives are defined by kindness and goodness, they point to the source of true goodness: God Himself! He alone is good (Mark 10:18). I want to be the woman who lives daily by the Holy Spirit's supernatural power, pursuing holiness while resisting the pull toward unkind judging.

GORGEOUS GOODNESS

Guys *will* take notice when goodness guides a girl's behavior. Joshua observed, "Samantha didn't try to sleep with me on our first date. Many other girls I had gone on dates with would spend hours talking about Jesus, and then try to have sex with me. The clincher for me with Samantha was I knew after spending a few hours in conversation, even if I put the moves on her, she would not have agreed. I could tell by the way she talked about Jesus and the Bible, her modest outfit and her body language. She gave me a short hug and would lean in to the conversation, but didn't initiate kissing or any other physical touch."

Jacob, too, is drawn by the beauty of goodness: "I am attracted to a girl's character and conduct. If she speaks, acts, dresses in a godly, mature, and intelligent manner. Serving. Humility."

One definition of *goodness* in the original language of the New Testament is "beautiful, lovely." Don't we all want to be described that way?

Not only will goodness make us attractive, but like other characteristics of the fruit of the Spirit, this trait also comes with a reward! Ruth's story of living out goodness and finding its reward is so cool, she has her own book in the Bible. You can guess its name: Ruth!

Ruth's story begins in the Middle East in her home country of

Moab. Because of a famine, some of God's people moved to Moab. Ruth, who was a Moabite, married into one of these Hebrew families, but before she had children, her husband died. Her father-in-law and brother-in-law died too! Her miserable mother-in-law, Naomi, packed up the family goods and prepared to head back to Israel. She encouraged Ruth to move back home with her own family. Ruth didn't grab this way out. Instead, she chose goodness. She put her mother-in-law's needs ahead of her own, promising to stay with her no matter what.

After they entered the city of Bethlehem, Ruth didn't sit back and assume Naomi would figure out what to do next. She selflessly worked hard in a field all day to provide food for the two of them.

That's when Boaz spotted her. "Boaz asked the foreman of his harvesters, 'Whose young woman is that?'" (Ruth 2:5). Hearing her story, he was impressed and paid her a compliment:

> I've been told all about what you have done for your mother-in-law since the death of your husband—how you left your father and mother and your homeland and came to live with a people you did not know before. May the LORD repay you for what you have done. May you be richly rewarded by the LORD, the God of Israel. (verses 11–12)

Continuing to show goodness, Ruth chose not to chase after guys (3:10). She followed the wise counsel of her mother-in-law. Her reputation for goodness became well known. In fact, according to Boaz, all the townsmen knew she was a woman of noble character.

Just as Boaz had said, God richly rewarded Ruth's goodness. Boaz married her, and she became the great-grandmother of King David and part of the family line that Jesus was born into! What an amazing blessing she received from choosing goodness! *And* she got her own book in the Bible too!

Proverbs 14:22 echoes the truth revealed in Ruth's story: "Those who plan what is good find love and faithfulness." I've found this to be true in my life! When I have chosen goodness, God's ways, I have been rewarded! With the power of the Holy Spirit living in me, He's helped me to make wise choices, living with few regrets. God helped me to write a story that I am happy to share with others—His story in me. Has it been easy? Definitely not. But living a life of goodness—rather than pursuing what makes me feel good in the moment—has brought me peace and God's blessings and favor. I would never trade His favor for the favor of a few fleeting friends.

I am confident the same will be true for you!

God, I want this magnetic characteristic of goodness. I want to live my life for the benefit of You and others, knowing that when I do, I am the one who truly benefits. I love You! Amen.

No Matter What

Learning Faithfulness

You would have thought Courtney and Carrie were sisters, they were so inseparable. Being new students on the first day of first grade, their awkwardness in their new school made them a perfect pair. All through elementary and middle school, nothing could push them apart. Trying new sports, creating cool outfits, making crazy videos—they enjoyed every aspect of their friendship.

After years of being close, though, they grew used to each other, so comfortable that they began taking their friendship for granted. Then Carrie found another girl, whose taste for offbeat music and sassy fashion Carrie found interesting. Gradually, she began spending more time with the new girl, and like an outdated phone, her best friend was replaced.

Courtney, of course, was wounded and lashed out. A rift grew between the former best friends, and by the time Carrie realized what had happened, her friend was gone for good.

Faithfulness is the superglue of relationships. But it's uncommon today as we chase after the latest and greatest rather than value what we already have. Carrie and Courtney's friendship fell apart because faithfulness was missing from their lives.

A faithful girl is loyal and constant, and can be depended on. David gives the perfect description of her in Psalm 15:

> Who may worship in your sanctuary, LORD? Who may enter
> your presence on your holy hill? Those who lead blameless
> lives and do what is right, speaking the truth from sincere
> hearts. Those who refuse to gossip or harm their neighbors
> or speak evil of their friends. Those who despise flagrant
> sinners, and honor the faithful followers of the LORD, and
> keep their promises even when it hurts. Those who lend
> money without charging interest, and who cannot be bribed
> to lie about the innocent. Such people will stand firm
> forever. (NLT)

I want to be this woman! She does what is right. Speaks the truth from her heart. She wouldn't talk behind anyone's back. She keeps all of her promises—no matter what!

Yet, when looking at my calendar, I'm challenged to not fill the days with me: my needs, my wants, my concerns. Afraid I'll become too busy and miss out on something, at times I hesitate to commit and be faithful.

With seven brothers and sisters, I find keeping in touch with all of them almost impossible. A few years ago, I made a New Year's resolution: every month I would contact each of them somehow. By March, I had already broken my vow. Why so fast? Distracted, I allowed new and "important" things to take priority over my faithfulness to my siblings.

Who do you see being faithful in your world?

....

....

....

When you look for examples of faithfulness, do your thoughts fill instead with stories of just the opposite? Your parent who walked out. The boyfriend who dumped you. Your best friend who grew tired of your problems. The youth pastor who burned out.

People let us down—they disappoint us. They are, after all, human.

God, however, cannot be unfaithful—ever. The Bible says, "For great is his love toward us, and the faithfulness of the LORD endures forever. Praise the LORD" (Psalm 117:2).

Since this same perfectly faithful God lives in us, we should find it natural to be true to Him and others. Why, then, are our hearts, as an old hymn says, "prone to wander"? Why do we wander from God and wander from relationships we value?

All too often the next big thing, that fascinating someone, or convenient alternative tempts us to choose fun over faithfulness. We must fight to be faithful. In Hebrews we find this promise:

God is not unjust; he will not forget your work and the love you have shown him as you have helped his people and continue to help them. We want each of you to show this same diligence to the very end, in order to make your hope sure. We do not want you to become lazy, but to imitate those who through faith and patience inherit was has been promised. (6:10–12)

Faithfulness is important to God; it needs to be important to us too!

Check Your Loyalty Level

Take this short quiz to see if faithfulness is already part of your character.

A) Your mom asks you to clean your bathroom before your aunt arrives. You...

    1. say "Sure" but never follow through.

    2. grumble a bit, finishing just as your guest arrives.

    3. get it done.

B) Your favorite band is coming to town. Your best friend asked months in advance to go with you. Now the guy you're crushing on invites you. You...

    1. say yes, then make up a story for your friend about why you can't go.

    2. ask your crush to join you and your friend.

    3. explain to your crush you have a commitment, then suggest a date the following weekend?

C) Your friend's in a cast, which makes swimming at your pool party impossible. You...

    1. leave her in the house with your parents.

2. help her down to the pool
area to watch the fun by
herself.

3. join her on the pool ledge
and enjoy watching your
friends have fun.

D) On vacation, you and your friend meet a couple
of guys. You're dating someone back home.
You...

1. forget all about your guy back
home.

2. hang out with them and flirt
just a little.

3. steer clear of the guys the rest
of the week.

How did you score?

10-12: Everybody would love to have you for a
friend!

7-9: It's a little iffy. Time to pay more attention
to your loyalty level.

4-6: Relationship with you is risky. Focus on
faithfulness.

Be sure to record your score in the chart in the
back on page 187. This will help you see which traits
are your strongest as well as where you need to
focus more!

THE HEART OF FAITHFULNESS

Jesus knew we would struggle to be faithful. He saw this struggle in some of His disciples. Knowing stories stick better than sermons, Jesus told the parable of the talents, found in Matthew 25:14–30.

A boss, in preparation for a journey, trusted his workers with his money while he was gone. "To one he gave five talents of money, to another two talents, and to another one talent, each according to his ability. Then he went on his journey" (verse 15).

While they weren't all given the same amount, each received something and was given the freedom to invest as he chose. "The man who had received the five talents went at once and put his money to work and gained five more. So also, the one with the two talents gained two more. But the man who had received the one talent went off, dug a hole in the ground and hid his master's money" (verses 16–18).

After a long time, the boss came back to find out what they had done with his money. "The man who had received the five talents brought the other five. 'Master,' he said, 'you entrusted me with five talents. See, I have gained five more.' His master replied, 'Well done, good and faithful servant! You have been faithful with a few things; I will put you in charge of many things. Come and share your master's happiness!'" (verses 20–21).

The conversation with the second guy was much the same. Wise choices and faithfulness resulted in doubling his money. "Well done" and all kinds of good came his way too (verses 22–23).

Guy Number 3? He freaked out. Worried he'd get into trouble if he lost the boss's money, he hid the gold in the ground. He was right about one thing: trouble was headed his way. Listen to his boss's response: "You wicked, lazy servant! So you knew that I harvest where I have not sown and gather where I have not scattered seed? Well then, you should have put my money on deposit with the bankers, so that when I returned I would have received it back with interest" (verses 26–27).

Because he chose the easy path instead of the right one, this guy lost everything. "Take the talent from him and give it to the one who has the ten talents. For everyone who has will be given more, and he will have an abundance. Whoever does not have, even what he has will be taken from him. And throw that worthless servant outside, into the darkness, where there will be weeping and gnashing of teeth" (verses 28–30).

As I read Jesus's story over and over, something struck me. Three men were entrusted with a valuable resource: money. Each of the first two guys "put his money to work." But the last guy, Scripture says, "hid his master's money."

Choosing the easy path instead of the right one could cost us everything.

The difference: the first two took ownership of the money, but Guy Number 3 continued to view the money as belonging to his master.

When I was younger, my parents often had to get on me to take care of their car, not spill on the rug, not waste the food they bought and cooked. But once it was my car, my clothes, or my money, I didn't want any of my stuff scratched, broken, or damaged. Ownership caused me to be more invested in taking care of things.

I think this translates to our faithfulness. When my faith was my mom's faith or my youth pastor's faith, I liked going to church because it meant hanging out with friends. When God became my Savior and my love—when my faith was truly my own—my perspective changed. Jesus became my everything. I don't want anything in my life that could scratch, break, or damage my relationship with Him! Nothing, absolutely nothing, is important enough to come between me and my Jesus.

The same is true for my other relationships. Those precious to me—my family, my friends, my teammates—deserve nothing less than my faithfulness. I want to be true to these relationships so nothing will break, scratch, or damage them. When I am faithful, when I invest in my relationships as the two faithful servants invested their master's money, I see my relationships grow stronger and deeper. I receive a return—and a reward.

In Jesus's parable, the giver of the talents rewarded each servant according to his faithfulness. The first two the master bragged on: "Well done, good and faithful servant[s]!" He invited them to even more of all he had. For the unfaithful servant, the master's words were harsh. "wicked" and "lazy," to be exact. What the servant had was taken away, and he was thrown out into the street.

Trustworthiness brings God's best, while untrustworthiness brings the worst. There's no middle ground. Faithfulness is a deal maker or deal breaker.

Nowhere is faithfulness more important than in our relationships. We need to wise up our wandering hearts. By following the direction of the Holy Spirit instead of chasing after the latest fad or impulse, we can train our hearts to be faithful, reaping the benefits. Our relationships will be stronger, more loving, more committed.

Faithfulness is a deal maker or deal breaker.

Faithfulness brings blessings to other areas of our lives as well. The girl who is faithful in small things—showing up for her commitments, keeping secrets secret, doing what she says she will do—this girl will be rewarded by our faithful God. That principle of sowing and reaping shows up again.

Remember the time you did an extra-great job cleaning? Your mom gave you more allowance! How about when you kept your commitment to baby-sit even though your friends tried to coax you to go to a movie instead? Now, you love that family; you're practically their nanny! Your friends encouraged you to stay out later, but you came home on time. Showing faithfulness and responsibility gained you an extended curfew! What about that time your best friend's heart was broken and you were there for her in the middle of the night? She's been there for you too! Faithfulness brings rewards.

 Describe a time or two when faithfulness eventually rewarded you.

. . . .

. . . .

. . . .

. . . .

. . . .

. . . .

When you're tempted to let go of something good in order to snatch at something seemingly better, think back on the times faithfulness paid off. Those memories can help you train your eyes and heart to be wise and go after what is good every time.

The Bible is loaded with stories of people God rewarded for their faithfulness:

- *Enoch.* "Enoch walked faithfully with God; then he was no more, because God took him away" (Genesis 5:24, TNIV). One day he was on the earth; the next he wasn't. He never died! I'd love that reward.

- *Noah.* "Noah was a righteous man, blameless among the people of his time, and he walked faithfully with God" (Genesis 6:9, TNIV). He and his family were spared from the flood that covered the entire earth.
- *Nehemiah.* He walked faithfully with God, and God allowed him to rebuild the walls of the city he loved (Nehemiah 13:14).

There are many, many more of God's faithful people listed in His Word. You can be on that list in God's eyes!

GODLY GUYS GO FOR FAITHFULNESS

When I asked Robbie, age eighteen, what he found attractive in a girl, his list included a great sense of humor, a sweet heart, love for her family, loyalty, truthfulness, and a heart devoted to God.

Of Robbie's six traits, four include aspects of faithfulness. Faithfulness also came into play when I asked him what he found unattractive: "One major turnoff for me is a girl dressed in anything too short or revealing. Immodesty shows she's begging for attention and doesn't have the confidence she needs to make a loyal girlfriend."

Who would have guessed immodesty is considered an indicator of potential unfaithfulness?

When Carlton told me about his fiancée, Jenna, faithfulness was the thing making his girl stand out. "Faithfulness is one characteristic that makes Jenna so different from other girls. I see this mainly in her walk with the Lord, but it also shows in how she rarely lets me down. When she tells me she is going to do something, she does. She's the most loyal person I know."

What a compliment! When I asked Jenna how she developed this depth of faithfulness in her life, she shared with me her powerful story of a heart transformed from desperation for attention to dependence on Jesus.

"I grew up in a Christian home with two very supportive parents," she said. "But in eighth grade a lot of girls had boyfriends and I wanted one too. So I started wearing makeup, dressing to attract guys, and becoming friends with the girls the guys liked. Sure enough, it worked; I got the attention I wanted. Throughout high school I dated, but not a single guy was a Christian. In my heart I always wanted a Christian guy to like me; I couldn't understand why they didn't. My senior year my boyfriend broke up with me because I wouldn't have sex with him. I realized then the guys I dated only stuck around long enough to get what they wanted. I was ready for a change."

Jenna took steps to make that change a reality. "I chose to stop focusing on guys and start focusing on the Lord. I stopped hanging out with the people who weren't following Him and spent my free time with friends who did. As I began spending time with Jesus in His Word and with other believers, He began to change my heart. Slowly I started weeding out my wardrobe, getting rid of immodest clothes, including my bikinis.

"For the first time in my life, I wasn't looking for a guy. As I was pursuing Jesus, I became friends with Carlton at church while hanging out in groups. I kind of liked him, but I didn't pursue him the way I would have before. I was pleasantly surprised when he asked me to dinner. For the first time a guy seemed attracted to me without me trying to attract him. In fact, it was the first time a Christian guy had been attracted to me at all!"

But even with a great guy showing interest in her, Jenna remained faithful to her first priority: her relationship with Jesus. "We spent a month praying for the Lord's will. Should we date each other? After thirty days, God still seemed to be leading us together, so we decided to officially date. Setting strict boundaries for our relationship, we guarded our hearts. Our commitment included not kissing each other except to say hello or good-bye and not telling each other we loved each other unless we got engaged. After three-and-a-half wonderful and fun-filled years, Carlton told me he loved me and wanted to be with me forever."

Jenna said yes to his marriage proposal! "I have never ever been treated with such absolute, sweet love and the utmost respect," she told me. "I could never have attracted a man like Carlton with the stupid measures I was using before. This love can only come straight from our Lord. Jesus had always been a part of my life, but it wasn't until He became my entire life that He brought my wonderful, amazing, beautiful husband into the picture."

> Know that the LORD has set apart the godly for himself; the LORD will hear when I call to him.
>
> **Psalm 4:3**

When I read Jenna's story, I think of Psalm 31:23: "Love the LORD, all his saints! The LORD preserves the faithful, but the proud he pays back in full." The word for "preserve" in the original Hebrew language means "to guard, protect, keep." That is exactly what the Lord did for Jenna and Carlton. As they were faithful to Him and to each other, He protected them, keeping them for His best.

CAN YOU BE TRUSTED WITH HIS HEART?

Jenna described how, before she focused her heart on Jesus, she would do whatever it took to get a guy's attention. So often guy/girl relationships are treated as a game—and someone ends up losing.

When you are dating a guy, do you think it is okay to flirt with other guys, call them, hang out with them? Why or why not?

. . . .

. . . .

. . . .

. . . .

. . . .

. . . .

Ever experience that little high when you flirt and get a guy's attention? That high is addictive. The more you flirt, the more you like the attention it brings. The more you like the intoxicating feeling, the more you'll look for it. The problem comes when it's time to commit to just one guy. If you're addicted to flirting, you might feel let down or even bored when you're limited to the attention of just your fiancé or husband, especially after you move past those early stages of the relationship. You've trained your emotions to seek out the emotional and physical responses that make you feel special,

Flirting can cause relationship failure; faithfulness proves his heart is safe with you.

wanted. The addiction can tempt you to flirt with other guys and risk relationship failure, because it can make your man question your faithfulness, even break his trust.

You want your guy to know you are a faithful girl and his heart is safe with you—he doesn't have to think twice or worry that you'll flirt with other guys. Remember that Proverbs 31 girl? "Her husband has full confidence in her and lacks nothing of value" (verse 11). Her man can trust her.

My friend Julie demonstrates that level of faithfulness. I asked her boyfriend to describe this amazing trait in her: "As I learn more about Julie, it's obvious that honesty and trust are very important to her. It made me feel I could trust my heart to someone who holds honesty so high. I believe it builds a stronger relationship both for true friendships and for those we date. If two people are far apart when it comes to honesty and faithfulness, that couple may find it difficult when they face obstacles in their relationship and situations that might naturally cause them to doubt each other.

"As I got to know Julie," he continued, "her faithfulness to God made me love her more. Her comments about God and her stories of how prayer helped her through life helped me trust who she is. Guys are visual; someone's faithfulness to God mirrors their faithfulness to others. As I observe people's actions, it tells me who they are. Julie's actions are consistent; she is a faithful girl."

Wouldn't you love to be described in those terms? I, too, want to be known as consistent, dependable, and faithful. I want my man to know that he can count on me always, no matter what.

FAITHFULNESS IN THE HARD STUFF

Determined to keep in shape all through the winter, my friend Tammy and I took the risk of running outside. Not too smart! After wiping out on the ice when we were over two miles from home, I was in trouble. My foot was nothing but dead weight, worthless. I couldn't put any pressure on it. But my faithful friend Tammy stuck with me as we walked those freezing miles home.

A relationship without faithfulness and trust is worse than my bum foot. It lacks a strong core to support it. If you don't have trust, the relationship has nothing to stand on.

Trust is built and reinforced when we prioritize honesty and truthfulness in our relationships. When you notice something happening that's not in the best interest of the person you love, do you care enough to go through some pain to preserve your rela-

If you don't have trust, your relationship has nothing to stand on.

tionship? If so, you'll choose to speak truthfully about a problem, even if it might offend or upset that person. With words motivated by love and marked by humility, you will talk about the painful or damaging issue.

To do that, you'll most likely have to turn your back on your fears, trusting the Lord with your anxious questions:

- *Will we break up if I reveal his teasing hurts me?*
- *How will she respond when I tell her I know she talked behind my back?*
- *What will he think if I tell him the truth about my standards?*

Faithfulness takes the risk in order to guard the relationship. When you decide to step out and speak truthfully, it will be uncomfortable. Confrontation can be downright scary. But I know from personal experience that having those hard conversations is a necessary part of faithfulness and a necessary part of healthy relationships with God, our loved ones, and ourselves.

Deciding to move forward with one such conversation with a boyfriend changed the course of my life. In only a few short months our hearts had gone from go-cart fun to NASCAR speed. We were moving so fast, our relationship was a blur. Though I had just turned eighteen, our goal was to get married—soon. Notice I said "our goal."

Through some wise advice from godly girls, I began to see our relationship for what it was. Though we both loved Jesus and were working to remain sexually pure, our top priority was each other. We each held the number one spot in the other person's heart, and it was wrong. I knew it was time to say good-bye, and so I did.

You may think it odd I would choose to tell a story of breaking up when we're studying faithfulness! But faithfulness was exactly the character trait I needed in order to break up. I needed to be faithful to God, to make Him my first love again. To be trustworthy and reliable to this guy I loved, I needed to set him free so that he could make God, not me, the center of his life. We each needed to turn to God as the source of our strength, hope, and future. Faithfulness chose the best: to let the relationship end.

PUTTING OUR FAITHFULNESS INTO ACTION

In most cases, of course, faithfulness means sticking with a relationship, especially in marriage. Matthew 19:4–6 makes this clear:

> "Haven't you read," he replied, "that at the beginning the Creator 'made them male and female,' and said, 'For this reason a man will leave his father and mother and be united to his wife, and the two will become one flesh'? So they are no longer two, but one. Therefore what God has joined together, let man not separate."

In a world where vows are broken easily, we demonstrate our faithfulness to God and others less by the words we choose and more by the actions we take.

Guests couldn't help smiling as they watched the fidgeting groom. The crowd stood as the bride glided down the aisle, gazing at her groom. The closer she got to her man, the more radiant she became. *Absolutely stunning!* I thought. I knew the groom had the same thoughts—and not just because it was his wedding day. Ron had sent me a note just a few days before the big event:

My and Kari's story started with trust and a prayer: "God, I want to meet someone who loves You as much as I do, her life based on her relationship with You above anything else." (I also told Him a bonus would be a natural beauty!)

Seeing Kari at church, I wasn't aware God was answering my prayers. Crossing paths with her as we volunteered, I started creating opportunities just to interact with her. As we talked, I saw she was not only beautiful, but very sweet. Texts, phone calls, and dates brought me to knowing Kari and loving her.

Early on I saw Kari's commitment in volunteering, but I had no idea how committed she was to the Lord. Seeing her joy when worshiping and her faithfulness in serving was extremely attractive to me. (I know it sounds a bit strange to be attracted to someone while watching them worship, but this was what I prayed for!)

God answered my prayers, giving me more than I asked. Faithful to wait for the right relationship and self-control to resist temptation enabled Kari to live a life of purity. She not only honored God; she has a gift to offer her future husband and an example for the middle-school girls she teaches.

As a woman who exhibits contentment and peace more than anyone I've ever known, Kari is so focused on being faithful to God she's not caught up in material pursuits and positions. This takes a lot of pressure off me! All these qualities drew me to Kari, the reasons I've fallen in love with her. I am incredibly blessed.

While Ron loved many beautiful traits in Kari, the first ones grabbing his attention were faithfulness, trustworthiness, and reliability, demonstrated through her actions.

What actions are the Holy Spirit leading you to take in order to make faithfulness one of your greatest traits? Proverbs 3:3 challenges us: "Let love and faithfulness never leave you; bind them around your neck, write them on the tablet of your heart."

Wrap up your time by describing very specifically one way you will show faithfulness to someone this week.

. . . .

. . . .

. . . .

. . . .

. . . .

. . . .

Let's not just talk about being faithful; let's do it!

Jesus, faithfulness is a quality so lacking in our culture. I want my life to be beautiful because of my faithfulness to You, my faithfulness to those I love, and my faithfulness to the commitments I make. With You and in You, I can do all things! Amen.

The fruit of the spirit is

Gentleness

A Tender Touch

Displaying Gentleness in a Harsh World

She might have been gentle, but man, could Lindsey kill a ball. Cheering for her and my daughter on the softball field was a highlight in my week. But who was the other lady in the bleachers? Rain or shine, one elderly woman showed up and kept her eyes on the field. She didn't yell, didn't smile, and didn't make much conversation either. It bugged me not knowing who she was! After nosing around, I discovered the "mean old lady," as she called herself, was Lindsey's grandma.

Grandma Joan had good reason to be mean; betrayal had beaten her down. Her husband went off to work one day—and never came back. Two small children were left to her total responsibility. After her husband went missing without a trace, she learned to be strong. And hard. Her demeanor was always blunt; she never minced words. Although she had come to know the Lord later in life, she always had an edge.

But that "mean old lady" bore little resemblance to the grandma that Lindsey loved. Every day after school, Linz snuggled up with Grandma Joan and shared the events of her day. The two were close buddies.

God knew Grandma Joan would need a buddy. Lung cancer inflicted her with baldness, frailty, and broken teeth. Yet Lindsey saw only the grandma she had always loved; her young heart swelled with gentle compassion for her grandmother's declining state. Nothing between them changed no matter how Grandma's body changed. God's life inside of Lindsey continued to gently pour out to her grandma.

Grandma Joan was already living with Linz's family when the cancer returned, incurable and inoperable this time. Lindsey's crushed heart knew their time together was limited. Every night she slipped into Grandma Joan's room, held her hand while sharing her day, and topped off the visit with a good-night kiss.

Lindsey was never severe or rough toward this person who was not naturally gentle. Her gentle spirit captured the heart of a "mean old lady" to create a precious friendship. Grandma Joan went to be with the Lord knowing she was unconditionally loved and would be forever remembered.

OUR GENTLE GOD

When I was in school, I always envied girls like Lindsey. The word *gentle* never described me. *Loud* was a better fit. Ever hear of someone put on probation at a Christian school for talking too much? You have now! *Too much* was often scribbled on my report card. That's what I heard, that's what I believed, and each year I only grew worse.

I began to think Talks Too Much was my name. Sixth grade brought a promotion: my teacher moved my desk right next to his! His tactic, intended to slow me down, only accelerated my mouth as embarrassment made me feel worse about myself. In seventh grade, promotion came with probation, my lack of self-control putting me on the list of students the teachers watched. That's when I really began to beat myself up. I viewed my exuberant personality as a liability. In middle school, aren't we just trying to figure out who we are and who others want us to be?

I'm sure at one time you have wished to be someone you weren't. In those years I wanted to be the quiet, feminine girl. Having friends who were soft spoken just made me wish I were more like them. I mistakenly thought gentleness meant soft spoken, petite, even fragile. Therefore I knew I could never be gentle! I didn't really understand this fruit of the Spirit. I just knew I was unhappy with my image of too much and too loud.

Maybe, like me, you naturally tend to be a bit on the loud side; you get down on yourself and try to stifle your natural exuberance. We don't need to! Being chatty and being gentle are not opposites. Jesus can empower us to be gentle while still being exactly the women He created us to be. Bold girls can be gentle too!

What I really needed, more than correction, was gentleness. If only someone had shown me the side of God the Bible calls Abba Father. Think Papa. Warm, kind, loving. Words I would not often have used to describe my father.

Working two jobs to provide for his family of eight kids meant my dad was rarely home. When he was, he was exhausted. But I treasure one faint memory swirling in my mind from when I was about six or seven. I remember Dad and me lying on the floor, watching *The Wizard of Oz,* his arm wrapped around me. When the Wicked Witch of the West appeared, even though I was terrified, I was safe. Dad was near.

Sometimes I still desperately need gentleness like that. Maybe you do too. Life can be a scary place, harder than we'd like. While my dad is no longer on this earth, I can picture myself wrapped up in God's warm father arms, soaking in His love, finding safety to calm my anxious mind and soothe my aching heart.

Are You a Gentle Soul?

Take a minute to assess how well you understand and share God's gentleness.

A) You can't find your straightener. Your sister has taken it again! Ready to yell at her, you find her crying in her room. You...

    1. yell at her anyway.

    2. walk away, aggravated.

    3. lie on the bed, holding her.

B) Your birthday is over and you didn't get the gift you wanted. You...

    1. are aggravated and quiz your parents about why you didn't get what you wanted.

    2. let your irritation show, then declare you'll buy it with your own money!

    3. show thankfulness and gentleness to those who remembered your birthday.

C) While serving in your city's soup kitchen, you notice some of the homeless have bad attitudes. You...

    1. give back some attitude as you hand out the food.

      2. point it out to your friend
         serving with you.

      3. continue serving with a gentle
         smile.

D) A freshman on the basketball team sits on the end of the bench, alone. You...

      1. sit near your buddies; she'll get
         over it.

      2. sit near the end so she isn't
         alone.

      3. sit next to her, extending
         friendship.

How did you do?

10–12 points: You're doing a great job at being tender toward others; keep showing Jesus to others!

7–9 points: Sometimes you're gentle. Ask the Holy Spirit to open your eyes to more opportunities!

4–6 points: You need an overhaul; God can do it!

Don't forget to record your score in the chart on page 187. This will help you see which traits are your strongest as well as where you need to focus more!

It's a rough world out there, isn't it? Overworked teachers. Overwhelmed parents. After a while, your heart might believe that's just the way it is with adults.

Not so with our heavenly Father! Never overworked or overwhelmed, He's all powerful. Nothing gets on His nerves or wears Him out, especially not us. Though our bodies grow up, we always remain His precious children. He doesn't look down on us or feel angry when we mess up. Instead, He smiles as the papa He is and bends down to help. Hosea 11:4 tells us He leads His people with ties of kindness and love. I love this: "To them I was like one who lifts a little child to the cheek, and I bent down to feed them" (TNIV).

When I lean in to the gentle side of God, I become gentle with myself and others.

When you read this description of God, can you feel His tenderness and gentleness? He bends down to us.

Like a father helping a child tie a shoe, He helps me tie an unraveling relationship.

As a father lifts a little one into a tree, He boosts me so I grow.

Taking my hand, He puts me on His shoulders when I grow tired.

Just talking to Father God and reading His Word, I sense His gentleness toward me. When I lean in to the gentle side of God, I become gentle with myself and with others.

SEE THROUGH JESUS-COLORED GLASSES

Jesus was particularly gentle toward the most vulnerable. He didn't disregard those some viewed as unimportant. Instead He treated as precious and valuable the poor, the children, and the elderly, in the same way that Lindsey responded to her grandma.

And when the disciples tried to shoo away those bringing the little children to Him, He didn't let them get away with it. Instead of pushing the little ones away, He commanded, "Let the little children come to me" (Matthew 19:14). He saw and met their need for tender love, and He asks us to do the same.

Like Jesus, I need to see those who need gentleness. Often I miss them, my attention going toward those who are right in front of me: in my house, at my work, on my social media. I have to slow down and notice the less visible, the overlooked, just as Jesus does!

Jesus also demonstrated gentleness toward the hurting, those whom others had decided were unworthy. In John 8 we read of His interaction with a woman caught in adultery. You know she wasn't living a life she was proud of; she probably felt overwhelmed by shame, barely hanging on to her last shreds of self-worth. The book of Isaiah describes the gentleness that Jesus, the Messiah, showed her and other wounded people: "A bruised reed he will not break, and a smoldering wick he will not snuff out" (Isaiah 42:3).

This woman had made a bad decision—well, probably many bad decisions. Yet He offered her, in the middle of her sin, forgiveness and compassion. Jesus doesn't kick a girl when she's down, like we sometimes do.

Like Jesus, the magnetic girl doesn't look down on others for their weaknesses or shortcomings. She takes herself out of the gossip circle. Secure and strong in her relationship with Jesus, she steps out of the drama, no matter what her friends choose to say. Humbly, she recognizes on any given day she is capable of the same sin as anyone else. Only Jesus keeps us on His path. He gives us His strength to care for the hurting, and His gentleness flows through us as we become the protectors of the vulnerable.

Gentleness Never Forces Its Way

When we're constantly moving, so busy we push ourselves beyond what we should, we can easily cross over into harsh. Gentleness gets lost when we're trying to make something happen—and getting an attitude if it doesn't. Jesus tells us, "Come to me, all you who are weary and burdened, and I will give you rest. Take my yoke upon you and learn from me, for I am gentle and humble in heart, and you will find rest for your souls. For my yoke is easy and my burden is light" (Matthew 11:28–30). By allowing ourselves to first experience His grace-filled help, we can take steps toward becoming the girl He wants.

Like many of our magnetic traits, gentleness goes hand in hand with another captivating characteristic: patience. Ephesians 4:1–2 puts these two together: "As a prisoner for the Lord, then, I urge you to live a life worthy of the calling you have received. Be completely humble and gentle; be patient, bearing with one another in love." Humility, gentleness, and love are not what surround those you meet who are hurting at school, at work, at home.

All around us we hear the shouts: "Think of yourself!" "Get what's yours." "Don't let anyone push you around." "You have one life to live; live it the way you want!"

Paul argues the opposite: You have one life. Live it in a way that counts for Christ! Gentleness is part of that life.

Make a list of actions that display gentleness in a life that is worthy of the calling you have received.

. . . .

. . . .

. . . .

. . . .

Make a list of actions that don't display gentleness.

. . . .
. . . .
. . . .
. . . .

Being gentle begins with seeing the difference between living the way we want or choosing God's way. Like the teapot on my stove, when the pressure of deadlines, demands, and disappointments builds up, I want to blow off some steam and let someone have it just to relieve stress. God is teaching me to literally stop, breathe in deep, and allow Him to fill me with His tenderness. Getting near God and allowing His Holy Spirit to flow through me prepares me to be a giver of tenderness even when I don't feel tender. That's who I want to be: compassionate and gentle like God.

Too often, I am the roughest when I am afraid or uncomfortable. Running far away from insecure me, I must choose to leave that girl behind. Jesus can take on every burden I feel, even the burden of self-doubt. David says, "Praise be to the Lord, to God our Savior, who daily bears our burdens" (Psalm 68:19). A key word in this verse is "daily." He is willing and wants to carry our trials every day! When I see an unfeeling or callous woman emerging from me, maybe I need to ask myself, *What burden am I trying to carry that I wasn't meant to?*

 Do you feel like you have a weight or a burden you are carrying? What overwhelms your heart?

. . . .
. . . .
. . . .
. . . .

Your list of burdens may include school pressure, sports stress, friend drama, or family friction. David named guilt as his problem: "My guilt has overwhelmed me like a burden too heavy to bear" (Psalm 38:4).

Whatever they are, Jesus wants to lift all your burdens from you, even the heaviest of guilt and shame. Remember, He said, "Come to me…I will give you rest." He invites you to take a beauty rest that will transform your soul.

GORGEOUS GENTLENESS

I know this magnetic pull is a real thing. Joshua told me he found Samantha attractive because of her "kind and gentle" nature.

Alex, a college sophomore, clearly thinks gentleness is gorgeous. He gave me a list of what he finds attractive in a girl:

- She loves Jesus with all of her heart, soul, and mind.
- She has a heart for people.
- She is humble yet grounded in her identity in Christ.
- She is gentle yet passionate.

Both Joshua and Alex are drawn to the magnetic fruit of the Spirit in the life of a girl: love, kindness, gentleness. Guys also are attracted to girls who let *them* live out the fruit of the Spirit in masculine ways.

Returning home from a late-night concert, three girls hopped aboard the downtown train. With no seats available, they grabbed the rail and prepared for the jerky start they knew was coming. "Here, take our seats," a couple of guys politely offered.

"That's okay!" two responded. The third girl graciously replied, "Thank you," and accepted the offered seat.

She knew it was important to let a guy be a gentleman. These guys weren't trying to put her down with their offer, saying she was weak. Just the opposite! They were being gentlemen, showing respect.

Strengthened by the certainty that she belongs to God, the magnetic girl confidently welcomes gentlemanly behavior toward her. Not only does she embrace the differences between guys and girls, she's happy about them! This confidence also allows her to let the guys do the finding.

At a family gathering I met Robert, my sister's nephew-in-law. I asked this single, college-age guy, "What are you looking for in a girl?"

He took no time to answer, "A girl who is comfortable with who she is. She isn't trying to be someone she's not. I'm still trying to find her."

Notice the words he used: "find her."

Check out this verse: "He who finds a wife finds what is good and receives favor from the LORD" (Proverbs 18:22).

Who does this verse say is doing the finding in the guy/girl relationship?

. . . .

. . . .

. . . .

. . . .

. . . .

The guy! He's the one searching out and finding you. The pressure is all on him. There's no need to worry you won't find a guy unless you are bold. The finding is not up to you! God created guys to go out and find a girl. Searching—the hunter instinct—is part of the makeup and design God built into guys. You can stop worrying; let God take over.

Should you make yourself available? Yes. Aggressive? No. Go ahead, start a conversation, but let the guy take it from there.

Gentle Words Are Like Honey

There is no place where gentleness—or lack of it—is more evident than in our words. So often the areas in which we are hardest on ourselves are the same areas in which we become harsh and judgmental toward others. A student who fights to maintain a high GPA puts down one who struggles academically. The girl continually working out has little sympathy for the overweight.

Those judgmental attitudes we inflict on ourselves poison our thoughts with negative feelings toward others as well. Remember what Anne said in chapter 7? "Since I hated my body   actually I hated myself—this made it easier for me to hate other people." Somehow we decide that others don't deserve grace and forgiveness since we don't give any to ourselves.

Criticized for a project that didn't turn out, I beat myself up. *Why didn't I do better? I could have slowed down, worked harder. What do they think of me now?* Discouraged and defeated, I fill up with negativity, oozing on to those around me. I find myself picking on their less-than-perfect qualities, finding fault. When I'm not gentle with myself, I am not gentle with others.

This is opposite of where we want to go. Proverbs 16:24 says, "Pleasant words are a honeycomb, sweet to the soul and healing to the bones."

Too often as Christians we are known for what we stand against rather than what we stand for. Yes, we want to avoid those things the Bible says are wrong, but more of our energy needs to be spent on doing the Jesus stuff! Loving the poor, speaking words of respect, showing tenderness to everyone.

Rather than harsh words of judgment, our conversation should be filled with light, life, and hope. First Peter 3:15 makes it clear: "Always be prepared to give an answer to everyone who asks you to give the reason for the hope that you have. But do this with gentleness and respect." We need never be ashamed to share our faith when we do so with gentleness and humility.

 When others shared their faith with you, were they gentle or judgmental?

. . . .
. . . .
. . . .
. . . .
. . . .

The way we speak to others makes all the difference in whether we will be heard and others will listen. Consider how God spoke to Elijah in 1 Kings 19:9–18. Elijah was on the run. He had just participated in one of the biggest miracles the Bible records, but now a witch of a woman was promising to kill him. Running for his life, he hid in a cave. There God came to speak with His discouraged prophet.

First came a wind so powerful, the mighty force shattered the rocks. But God didn't speak to Elijah in the powerful wind. Next came an earthquake, shaking the mountain. God wasn't in the earthquake either. A fire followed, but that wasn't God. Lastly came a gentle whisper. God spoke.

God didn't choose to be dramatic or forceful, as Elijah might have expected. Instead God tenderly whispered the words He needed Elijah to hear.

Like God, the magnetic girl doesn't have to make a scene in order to be heard or noticed. She doesn't judge others, calling them out. She has no need to shock others with her words, her wardrobe, or her womanhood. She takes her cue from God.

Sometimes a whisper speaks loudest of all.

Fuel the Fire or Cool Things Down?

As you become who God wants you to be, your standard for what is okay and what is not may be different from that of others. Not that you're better than anyone else, but your behavior code is written by your heavenly Father, not by whatever emotion you currently feel. Your brain may yell, *Tell her off!* or *Give him what he deserves!* But the Holy Spirit living in you whispers, *Choose gentleness.*

In James 3:6 we read of the danger that comes when we don't listen to the Spirit's whisper but let our harsh words fly: "And the tongue is a flame of fire. It is a whole world of wickedness, corrupting your entire body. It can set your whole life on fire, for it is set on fire by hell itself" (NLT).

Pride-filled words stoke the fires of frustration, fueling an ember into a blaze of anger and destroying relationships. Proverbs 15:1 reminds us "a gentle answer turns away wrath." By carefully choosing our words, we avoid burning others. We can talk over problems without wrecking our relationships.

Think of the last fight you had. What words did you use to communicate how you felt? Were they gentle or harsh?

. . . .
. . . .
. . . .
. . . .

In the end, did your relationship come out better or worse?

. . . .
. . . .
. . . .

I'm not talking about avoiding confrontation. As we saw in the chapter on faithfulness, sometimes difficult conversations are necessary. But we can confront without setting our relationships on fire!

Fire prevention begins in the mind. You must determine, no matter what, you will always fight fair. Swearing, cussing, belittling, and name calling are out of bounds in an argument. Keep your conflicts classy! Carefully choose your words. Your opponents expect an insult for an insult. Gentleness will blow them away!

James gives us wisdom for gentle, healthy confrontation: "My dear brothers, take note of this: Everyone should be quick to listen, slow to speak and slow to become angry, for man's anger does not bring about the righteous life that God desires" (James 1:19–20).

Keeping our conflicts classy isn't just a good idea; we're *commanded* to avoid backbiting and bickering. Paul described the standard for Christ followers: "They must not slander anyone and must avoid quarreling. Instead, they should be gentle and show true humility to everyone" (Titus 3:2, NLT).

Keep conflict classy! Carefully choose your words.

Let's break it down. Paul used two words that are very important in understanding this verse: "must not." We must not slander. Not "We shouldn't." Nor "Try not to." The language here is straightforward, with no other options: We're commanded not to injure another person's reputation under any circumstances. Not if it's true. Not if they hurt me first. Not if they deserve it.

What a tough command! But here again we have to remember the principle of sowing and reaping. Obedience now brings blessing later!

Paul repeated that word "must" in the same sentence: we "must avoid quarreling." Again, when it comes to our argumentative discussions, we can choose words that stoke the fire or words that put it out.

Paul says we should be gentle and show true humility. We don't think we are any better than anyone else or that we are always right. This gentleness is not reserved just for our friends, our family, and those who don't get on our nerves, but is shown to everyone. You can choose to be gentle to the annoying girl on your team, the brother always demanding the remote control, and the classmate who constantly tries copying off your paper.

Will it be easy? No! Your feelings may scream, and your blood might boil. You'll be tempted to lose your temper and let someone have it.

To be humble, gentle, and patient requires strength, the supernatural kind. That's why Paul urges us to "let the Holy Spirit guide your lives. Then you won't be doing what your sinful nature craves" (Galatians 5:16, NLT). The ability to exercise gentleness comes from His Spirit in us, which is why we cannot take credit for it. These traits do not come into our lives because we work hard at being a good person. They indicate Jesus's life in us.

If I were to send you a text with a photo of my journal, you would see this verse I pray every day: "He guides the humble in what is right and teaches them his way" (Psalm 25:9). I know, on my own, I drift toward pride. I have to be humble so I can receive God's guidance every day.

I want others to look at my life and not say "Lynn is a good person" or "She must be a saint." In fact, if comments like those are the best it gets, I've failed! I want my life, every day, to be a living, breathing example of a life transformed by the power of God.

Remember, we are not our own; because of the choice we willingly made to be His, we don't get to decide how we act. Notice how Paul started Ephesians 4:1–2: "As a prisoner for the Lord, then, I urge you to live a life worthy of the calling you have received. Be completely humble and gentle; be patient, bearing with one another in love." Prisoners don't get to call the shots.

As you follow this calling, as you live *a life worthy* of it, you will be the whisper amid the noise, the quiet beauty that stands out in the crowd. Humble, gentle, patient, loving. These adjectives will not describe many of your peers. They are true only for the magnetic girl.

No, you can't live a perfect life, and yes, you will sometimes make mistakes. But you can be a girl who wakes up each day surrendering in a fresh way to letting the Holy Spirit display His gifts through you!

Today, find moments to intentionally be gentle. Like a spy on a mission, look for opportunities. Read your little sister a book. Carry groceries for an elderly neighbor. Respond calmly to the person who yells at you. Choose not to engage in a fight. Choose gentleness.

Jesus, by myself, I just don't have what it takes to be gentle. Left to myself, I continually speak my mind, even when it can hurt others. I am not gentle with others when I am not gentle with myself. I am not gentle with others when I think too highly of myself. I am not gentle with others when I don't see others as You do. But, Jesus, when I see the gentle side of You, I am able to be gentle with myself and with others. Thank You, Holy Spirit, for living out Your gentleness in me! Amen.

Keeping Your Cool

Seeking and Finding Self-Control

He could have been named Flash. Dave's running ability got him the attention he wanted, and if anyone missed his athleticism, he drew them in with charisma, charm, and good looks. His fast moves were not restricted to the track. One look from him and most girls melted like butter in the hot sun.

Knowing all the right things to say, he said them to Terri, who soaked in his attention. Terri wanted everything a boyfriend like Dave could give her. "I thought I could have some fun with this guy," she later told me. "I was tired of doing what I thought was right in life: church, youth group, making a good impression for my parents who were so involved in church. This guy would make me really popular."

But she got more out of this relationship than she expected.

"One of the first nights we were together alone, he wanted to get physical more than I did, his exact words being, 'If you don't want to do this, I'll take you home and go out with my friends.' I was terrified, but didn't listen to my fear. I wanted to keep this awesome guy, so I did what he wanted. There was something about being wild, doing something I knew was wrong. I couldn't wait to I tell my friends I was finally his."

So Terri gave in, gave herself to him. Immediately afterward he took her home and went out with his friends anyway.

Within a short time, Dave was showering attention on a different girl. While Terri was still picking up the pieces of her shattered heart, she had to face another painful reality. "Never in my life did I expect to get a call saying 'It's positive' from Dr. Jeffries. My next call was to Dave. I sat on my bed as silence hung on the other end of the phone. Finally he demanded, 'Well, what are you going to do now?'

"I hardly remember the rest of the phone call. My mind was spinning. *Pregnant? Me pregnant? Having a baby? Dave won't stand by me; he's even with someone else now. How do I tell my mom and dad? How disappointed are they going to be in me? What will my church friends think? What an embarrassment I will be! How will I ever face anyone?*"

The consequences of giving up her self-control and giving in to Dave left Terri reeling. "I did whatever the guy had wanted because I thought that's how I could keep him. But to him I was just another girl. I had thought I would be so happy, feel amazing because I was being bad, crazy, throwing caution to the wind. All I felt was empty, guilty, hurt, ashamed, embarrassed, fooled, and pregnant.

"My life changed forever."

⸘⸘⸘⸘⸘⸘

Terri was so vulnerable in sharing her story with me because she hopes it will persuade other girls to change their lives while they can, to choose what is best by making wise choices. Her prayer is that her story will help others avoid the pain she experienced.

Though you may not have yet struggled with sexual pressures and temptation, we all struggle with self-control in some area. To identify some common areas in which young women wrestle with their impulses, I took a little poll. You couldn't call this scientific research or anything. I just asked a few girls this question: "What would you say are the areas in which girls struggle the most when it comes to self-control?"

Their answers confirmed one truth: some things never change. From the beginning of time, it seems, the same types of issues tempt us women to act carelessly and to sometimes take risks with our future:

- comparison
- jealousy
- guys
- words

What is the area in which you struggle the most to practice self-control?

. . . .
. . . .
. . . .
. . . .

The same things you struggle with, I struggled with as a young woman. Some I still struggle with today. All these troubles have their roots in the same place: our thoughts. So let's dive in to consider why we are tempted to do and say things that land us in trouble—and how we can better exercise self-control for our benefit and for that of others.

First, let's take our final quiz.

Taking Control
or Losing It?

Answer the following questions to see how successful
you are at keeping your cool under pressure.

A) Gym this semester includes two weeks of swimming. Dressing out in the locker room, you...

   1. make fun of another girl to hide
      your own insecurity.
   2. allow your mind to ridicule your
      body; you don't look like *her.*
   3. rein in your thoughts, get your
      swimsuit on, and get in the pool.

B) You've been crushing on a guy all summer. You
see on Twitter his new girl is your old best friend.
You...

   1. subtweet a nasty comment.
   2. call a friend to talk about why
      your old best friend is all wrong
      for him.
   3. ask the Holy Spirit to help you
      move on.

C) Your new crush asked you to the movies. Then you
find out he's planned an evening at his house—and
his parents won't be home. You...

    1. can't wait to get there!

    2. ask if he wants to go to the theater instead.

    3. realize he's not the guy for you and make new plans with a friend.

D) Your sister accused you of ruining her new shirt. You...

    1. call her liar and slam the door.

    2. walk out of the room while she screams at you.

    3. ask if there is any way you can help her fix it.

How did you do? If you got...

    10-12 points: You're practicing self-control already! Keep going!

    7-9 points: You're somewhat inconsistent. Keep your eyes open for opportunities to exercise your self-discipline muscles.

    4-6 points: Do you often feel out of control? The Holy Spirit can help!

Be sure to record your score in the back of the book, so you can identify your strengths as well as the areas where you need to seek God's help.

What's the Problem?

Before you can begin to address your own personal struggle with self-control, you'll have to get specific about what it is and why it's a problem. It's a bit like diagnosing and treating an illness.

Mariah spent far too long suffering from stomachaches. Finally, sick and tired of being sick and tired, she went to the doctor to find out what was wrong. The diagnosis was clear. Turns out, what is good for others isn't good for Mariah. Wheat, milk, and sugar actually make her sick. The solution was simple but far from easy: cut these ingredients from her diet.

Now that she has a name for her problem, Mariah has to make choices about everything she eats. What tastes good in the short term may make her feel bad in the long term.

She has to redesign her life, make changes leading to a healthy body. She's discovered what foods are wrong for her. She has to determine which alternatives are right. When Mariah decides to follow through, she feels so much better! One wise decision after another gets her feeling better!

In order to make wise choices on the spot, when temptation whispers, *Just one cookie,* Mariah has to retrain her brain. She has to fix the mix—not just the mix of foods she's eating but the mix of thoughts she allows to guide her actions. She exchanges thoughts like *You deserve this treat* for *You want to feel good!*

Design a New Direction

Whatever our own area of struggle, we too have to retrain our brain. We need to trade impulsive "I want it now" behaviors for the captivating characteristic of self-control. Like Mariah, we design a new direction for our lives as we...

- discover
- determine
- decide

While this list seems simple, self-control is anything but easy. We can trust the Holy Spirit, though, to provide the direction we need.

Following Mariah's pattern, let's design our own plan to gain self-control. Along the way, plug your self-control struggle into each step of the pattern to make it personal and practical.

In what areas do you struggle most when it comes to self-control?

. . . .

. . . .

. . . .

. . . .

Step One: Discover

When it comes to your greatest struggle, why do you think you are so tempted? Fill in the blanks to discover the underlying problem.

I want . . . .

so that . . . .

. . . .

. . . .

For example, you might write,

- *I want that boyfriend so that I have someone to love me.*
- *I want her body so that I feel confident.*
- *I want to say what's on my mind, so that I can know my opinions matter to others.*

If you didn't fill in the blanks, go back and do it now. Take a look at your sentence. Did filling in this sentence help you identify the root or the cause of your temptation?

As I mentioned earlier, the self-control issues listed in my unscientific poll had one thing in common: They begin with what we think. Whether we're comparing our bodies or daydreaming about the guy in class, uncontrolled thoughts can be a huge trap. Overcoming these traps begins with discovering why we think what we think.

Take, for instance, the temptation to compare. For me, it's all wrapped up in my thoughts about what other people will think of me: *Is my outfit right? Will they like me? Will they think I am good enough? Compared to her, do I have what it takes? What about my hair, my weight? Did I say that right?*

In completing the sentence above, then, I would say, *I want to compare so that I feel better about myself.* This implies I don't feel good about myself already. My comparison, then, is rooted in insecurity.

Step Two: Determine

Once we've discovered why we're falling for the temptation, we can determine to honor God no matter what. We conquer our out-of-control thoughts with truth. The determined mind is a powerful mind. We determine to trust the Lord to fulfill the desire that drives our problem thoughts and behaviors, including...

- the desire to know and feel loved.
- the desire to feel confident and good about who I am.
- the desire to know others care about what I have to say.

God has everything we need because He has it all: "For the world is mine, and all that is in it" (Psalm 50:12). If we truly need something, He will provide. We don't have to go after what we want, giving in to temptations that lead to trouble. Instead, we can determine to turn to God and ask Him to meet the longing prompting our out-of-control behaviors.

God knows you intimately. He knew when He created you what gifts, body, and life would be best for you. In Jeremiah 1:5 God says, "Before I formed you in the womb I knew you, before you were born I set you apart." He can be trusted to meet your needs!

Step Three: Decide

Now we must decide to follow through. Letting God satisfy our heart hunger rather than reaching for what looks or sounds amazing helps prevent regrets.

This is the hard part, the part where you will fail unless Jesus does it in you. That sounds so discouraging, I know. But it's not discouraging when you realize all our hope is wrapped up in Jesus! When we are the weakest, He is the strongest (2 Corinthians 12:9–10).

In fact, accepting your weakness helps you be more dependent on Him, making room for His supernatural strength. You can win! Through Him you are strong enough to win...

- the battle saying no to sexual temptation now, so you can have the best sex later.
- the struggle to find comfort in food, so you can be healthy.
- the fight against your addiction, so you can experience freedom.
- any conflict that tempts you to choose less than God's best for your life.

Let's take an in-depth look at several areas where we tend to need more of God's strength to overcome our natural urges with self-control: the urge to chase after more, the urge to speak careless words, and the urge to follow our feelings.

Control over Our Desire for More

Fourth grade is when the *mores* moved in—when my close friend got *the* pants and I didn't. That was the year my heart drew a line between the haves and the have-nots.

 Can you describe a time when you felt what you had wasn't enough? Is there an area where that's true for you right now?

. . . .

. . . .

. . . .

. . . .

The desire for more, whether it is more guys, better grades, or cooler garb, fuels temptation. More never gets enough; it always wants more. As soon as we get what we want, we find something more we "need."

We are constantly bombarded with all the reasons we shouldn't be content. Advertisers play on our insecurities about everything from yellow teeth to outdated phones, pushing emotional buttons to get us to buy. Research shows that we see 247 advertisements a day telling us we need more![5]

Their plan is to strip us of contentment so we'll seek fulfillment in things and experiences; but our deepest desires are never satisfied, even after getting the clothes and the car.

Jesus told us how to escape the desire for more: "Do not worry, saying, 'What shall we eat?' or 'What shall we drink' or 'What shall we wear?' For...your heavenly Father knows that you need them. But seek first his kingdom and his righteousness, and all these things will be given to you as well" (Matthew 6:31–33).

Wait, isn't this verse still talking about seeking more?

Absolutely, but the more that Jesus encourages us to seek is different from the never-ending craving for more stuff and status, as Mariah discovered on a missions trip.

When we arrived at the airport and found her there waiting, I could see Mariah was spent. Yet she had a twinkle in her eye. Her heart was so full. "I want to move to Costa Rica. The people there have so little, yet they are so happy. Life is slow and peaceful."

The next day, she could barely bring herself to return to her job at the country club. I couldn't blame her. She'd discovered the more Jesus offers: more peace, more purpose.

When we practice self-control and seek God's kingdom first, the *mores* of discontentment are silenced! The drive to do things we shouldn't do lessens, and our sense of gratitude increases. Research tells us that people who express gratitude feel 25 percent happier. They are more optimistic about the future and feel better about their lives.[6]

Can you even imagine how attractive a content girl is to a guy? A girl who practices self-control over materialism? A girl whose life isn't based on her next trip to the mall or getting those must-have shoes? Contentment settles his fears. No need to worry he won't be able to give her the stuff she wants because she already has all her needs met through God!

Now that we've *discovered* the wrong thoughts feeding the *mores* and we've *determined* God alone can satisfy our hunger, let's *decide* to seek His kingdom and righteousness—and be thankful for whatever He brings our way.

CONTROL OVER OUR MOUTHS

In my survey about the areas in which girls struggle for self-control, many answers had to do with words. For example:

- filtering my thoughts; saying everything on my mind is not necessary
- holding back things I want to say but probably shouldn't
- anger, yelling during disagreements

These comments remind me of a quote I once heard: "A fool empties her head every time she opens her mouth." I don't want to be a fool! The Bible makes it clear, though, saying everything we think gets us in trouble: "The wise in heart accept commands, but a chattering fool comes to ruin" (Proverbs 10:8).

Chattering certainly describes many of us. Dr. Louann Brizendine, clinical professor of psychiatry at the University of California, San Francisco, stated in her book *The Female Brain,* "Men use about seven thousand words per day. Women use about twenty thousand."[7] All those words…so many opportunities to say the wrong things!

Here's where we make our plan for self-control:

Discover. Why do we feel the need to talk so much? Are we processing externally what should be processed internally? Do we simply enjoy hearing ourselves talk?

In what situations or on what topics do you catch yourself talking more than you maybe should?

. . . .
. . . .
. . . .
. . . .
. . . .

Determine. We can choose to filter our words by examining our thoughts. We can't control what quickly passes through our minds, but we can control what we do with those thoughts. Determine to slow down; think before you talk. Proverbs 14:3 tells us, "A fool's talk brings a rod to his back, but the lips of the wise protect them." Self-control will save us from ourselves!

Decide. We can decide that we will use our words for good. Our mouths can be our most attractive feature! Words of encouragement, kindness, gentleness create a more beautiful you!

The girl who holds back when it comes to her tongue completely stands out. As Parker observed, "We don't need to know all of your emotions on social media! Please use social media as a tool, not a venting session or a selfie poster board." I'm guessing he feels pretty strongly; he put his answer in all caps!

There's definitely a place to bare your heart; the Internet is not that place. Expressing whatever passes through your brain is the norm, but we don't want to be normal. If you want your words to be magnetic, tell a guy what he wants to hear. Surveys tell us the most important thing to a guy is respect.[8] Notice I didn't say being loved; that's a girl thing.

Use your words to draw others to you, not drive them from you.

Guys are all about R-E-S-P-E-C-T.

When a guy takes a wrong turn, don't show off how smart you are. Respect him for finding his own way. If your boyfriend uses the wrong word, don't correct his grammar. Hard? You bet! We're smart, but too often we shove our intelligence in their faces and shove the relationship out the door! Nobody—especially a guy—likes a know-it-all.

Does this mean you act like you have no brain, no opinion, no strength? No way. It means you respect and admire his while resting confidently in your own. There is a time and place to respectfully give your opinion, but we don't have to give it on every subject every time. Ask

God for the wisdom to show you when you should hold back and when you shouldn't.

Proverbs 12:18 says, "Reckless words pierce like a sword, but the tongue of the wise brings healing." You show wisdom when you exercise self-control over your words and encourage your guy rather than cutting him down. When you're impressed, say so out loud. When he offers to help, allow him to! Respect his masculinity.

Even as I write that, I feel compelled to confess this is an area where God is still working to teach me wisdom.

As a girl who grew up in Iowa, if I don't get my snow fix at least once a winter, I'm just not right. Since I now live in the South, that fix doesn't always happen on its own, so a few years back we scheduled a snow-tubing trip to the Blue Ridge Mountains. After hauling all our gear plus family and friends up the mountain, we found ice, not snow, glistened on every surface. No way did we want my truck ice skating on the slope up to the mountain house, so my husband wisely parked at the bottom of the drive. He asked me to wait while he took our belongings up on foot, then he'd come back to help me safely to the top.

With a whole lot of laughter and a little bit of fear, I watched Greg inch his way up the incline. And that's when my thoughts took a danger-ous direction: *What am I doing sitting here while Greg risks his life? What kind of wimpy girl am I?* I was done watching and waiting. I thought I could help Greg and get us settled faster. As soon as he was out of sight, I began my ascent, dragging my suitcase along. Seconds later, feet flying through the air, I plummeted back to my truck.

"Why wouldn't you just wait? You could have broken something!" Greg yelled down to my bottom-up self.

Yes, I have some issues with restraint. Climbing things I shouldn't, going where others wouldn't, my tendency toward independence plus my adventurous spirit get me in trouble sometimes. Wow, do I need God's wisdom!

How attractive am I to my man when I fail to pause and ask God to filter my thoughts before I act? Not very. That day when I slid down the drive, Greg was definitely frustrated, even a little angry with me. Because I chose independence instead of respecting his judgment, I put myself in a place of danger.

I know I'm not the only one who struggles. But as Isaiah said, "There are still gentlemen out there! Chivalry isn't dead (yet)! Don't get so caught up in being a 'strong and independent woman' you never give a guy the chance to open the door or help you carry something heavy. A quote I really like says, 'I often wonder if girls were to act like ladies, if it would challenge boys to act like gentlemen.'"

CONTROL OVER OUR FEELINGS

When it comes to challenging our guys to act like gentlemen, self-control on our part goes a long way toward helping a godly guy keep his com-
mitment to purity. But that self-control needs to be designed into your plans far ahead of time, long before you even start talking to the guy. With the help of the Holy Spirit, you have to decide beforehand you will not put yourself in situations where your emotional and physical purity can be seduced.

Self-control says no to situations where your standards can be seduced.

At age thirteen, I discovered, deter-mined, and decided. I discovered my heart desperately wanted to feel wanted. I deter-mined I would answer that longing in Jesus and not in the arms of a boy. I decided to remain pure, in my thoughts and with my body, to honor God and protect the gift of my heart and body. That meant the guys I dated wouldn't have all of me.

Here was the standard I set to keep my virginity: no guy was going to touch or see under my clothes until after we said "I do" in a wedding ceremony. That went for him; it went for me.

Why, you may wonder, would I suggest you decide this even before you're in a relationship? The longing to love and be loved is extremely powerful; it will take over your best intentions unless you *discover* the love your heart craves first comes from Jesus. His love is the only love that will completely fill your love-starved heart. Once you *determine* to go to your Creator for the love only He can offer, then any guy He brings into your life is an added bonus! The key to maintaining self-control, no matter what your guy says or does, is to *decide* ahead of time to fill your heart with Christ's love.

Until and unless we are Jesus filled, we're too vulnerable to withstand the pressures of a relationship. Remember how we talked about our wandering heart? If we aren't already satisfied with Christ's love, our feelings can easily overpower and crush us. We'll find it nearly impossible to resist the pressure to compromise, to recalculate where we'll draw the line in our physical relationship. Temptation to do whatever it takes to get and keep the relationship going may prove too powerful to a heart not already confident in Jesus's faithful love.

Maybe you're wondering why this is such a big deal for some girls. *I just don't understand why girls struggle so much,* you think. *Just say no.*

You're right; saying no is easy. Until the feelings take over. Sweaty palms, feeling giddy, super happy! When you are around him, you just can't stop smiling. You want this feeling to last forever.

Infatuation is a bit like a roller coaster. You don't really know what it's going to be like until you experience it for yourself. Sitting in the cart, you feel anxious. Everyone else said it's fun; you believe them. The car starts pulling. Up, up, up. At the top you can see for miles, the whole park at your feet! Everything looks so different from this perspective.

Heart pounding, your anxiety builds. Then suddenly, down, down, down! As the wind flies through your hair, you're terrified but exhilarated.

And then it's over. The ride was far too short. So you get back in line to do it again. You've got to experience the thrill once more.

Soon the kiddie coaster feels a bit too boring, predictable. You move on to the wooden coaster. And then your friend persuades you to try the ultimate coaster, where all the screams are coming from. Adrenaline flowing through your body gives you boldness you never had before, convincing you to do what seemed unthinkable just a short time ago.

The desire to re-create and increase the feelings of excitement drives us to set aside our self-control. The pulsing of passion feels good. Our mind thrills to the whispered thoughts: *Somebody likes me. Somebody wants me. He thinks I'm beautiful and funny. He wants to be with me. He loves me!* If we add *I think this is "the one"!* the pressure increases all the more.

Remember how Terri talked about feeling wild, throwing caution to the wind because she thought Dave liked her? Trouble comes when feelings-driven thoughts overrule God's wisdom-living words.

> Trouble comes when feelings-driven thoughts overrule God's wisdom-living words.

Feelings are not bad; in fact, they're very good! God gave us these feelings to enjoy, to lead us into a relationship where one day we will be known and can fully know another. But the experience of fully knowing and being known is meant for after we are married.

We have to decide up front, before feelings explode: *Nothing and nobody is going to come between me and my Jesus! No need I have for affection. No screaming emotions or hormones. And most of all, no guy who can't possibly fill my desperate heart!*

Nothing—absolutely no guy or good time—is ever worth damaging our relationship with Jesus! We can't go against God and not receive negative consequences. As my friend Lysa TerKeurst says, "Sin and consequences always come as a package deal."[9]

When we make a right relationship with God our top priority, it will guard our lives. Instead of following what feels good, what seems fun, or what we think we deserve, we can be guided by His wisdom and the desire to bring Him honor.

While times have changed and our society is saturated with sexual images and suggestive language, our bodies have not. Since the beginning of time, the Creator has always known what's best for you. His standard for purity isn't to prevent you from having fun but to protect you from pain.

The choices I make today determine the course of my tomorrows.

Remember, the magnetic girl is intentional about fixing the mix when it comes to her thoughts. Culture says, *You're only young once. Get all you can get now. Live in the moment.* Wisdom, the voice of self-control, whispers, *The choices I make today determine the course of my tomorrows.*

Yes, temptation seems to be everywhere, but the Spirit gives you the strength to live out self-control. "The temptations in your life are no different from what others experience. And God is faithful. He will not allow the temptation to be more than you can stand. When you are tempted, he will show you a way out so that you can endure" (1 Corinthians 10:13, NLT).

How do you get out of temptation that feels like more than you can take? Be smart about your situation. Make the decision not to sit in a parked car, not to be together on a couch alone in the dark, not to be horizontal together. As Proverbs reminds us, "Discretion will protect you, and understanding will guard you" (2:11). Set the standard now and live it out when temptation comes, leaning on Him for help. For if we are not intentional about where we are going, we are sure to end up where we don't want to be.

There is a reason some of our body parts are called sexual organs: they are made for sex! Since the best sex is after we say "I do," those body parts are meant to be reserved for that day! We can try lying to ourselves, relabeling actions if we want. I can grab a can of motor oil, heat it in a mug, and call it hot chocolate, but it's still motor oil—and drinking it can kill me.

> If we are not intentional about where we are going, we are sure to end up where we don't want to be.

You can call the things you want to do anything but sex, but calling it something different doesn't change the reality that it can still kill your heart.

Joshua appreciated that Samantha understood this: "After I decided to take Jesus's commands in the Bible seriously, my criteria changed to dating girls who were Christian. When I met Samantha, she was the first girl I'd met who was okay with me calling sin, sin, agreeing sexual sin was not okay. She wanted to work together to not sin. She didn't condone it in our relationship."

The magnetic girl says, "My heart and my body are too valuable to give away to anyone under any conditions until after I share his last name."

GREAT JOY IS WITHIN REACH

You may have read this chapter thinking, *Too late! I've already blown it! I might as well keep heading in the wrong direction.*

So not true, my friend!

Remember Terri, whose story you read at the start of this chapter? She found herself in a seemingly impossible situation after giving in to her boyfriend's pressure. But even then, it was not too late. I'll let her tell you what happened as she weighed her choices.

"I knew two girls in my church who had gotten pregnant. One had had two abortions. The other girl was just sixteen and kept her baby. Whenever I would see her, I thought, *She can never do anything. She has so much responsibility now. She's so young, but her life is over.*

"I had a big decision to make. I asked my mom and dad what I should do, and they prayed with me. I knew I could not get an abortion. This child was at no fault and deserved to have the life God planned for her. I knew from having a relationship with Jesus, He did not make mistakes and no life is a mistake.

"After much soul searching and praying I made the decision to search for a Jesus-believing family to adopt my child, a couple who loved God and could not have children of their own. This baby was a gift, and I could give that gift to a family and give my baby a gift of a loving mother and father.

"When I went into labor, my parents were with me all the way; I had a baby girl. The adoptive parents were waiting somewhere private in the hospital. I never faltered on my decision, and God gave me a great peace.

The new youth pastor in our church came to see me in the hospital. I had not met him yet, but he reached out to me with love and acceptance. He wrote this verse on the board in my hospital room: 'Brothers, I do not consider myself yet to have taken hold of it. But one thing I do: Forgetting what is behind and straining toward what is ahead, I press on toward the goal to win the prize for which God has called me heavenward in Christ Jesus' (Philippians 3:13–14).

"This is what I am striving for every day in my life."

Terri wrapped up her story by saying, "There is no greater joy in life than living how you know God wants you to live. I would encourage every girl, give yourself to Jesus. He is where you will find true love, self-esteem, peace with yourself, and happiness. When you do, the only limit is the sky."

Terri went on from that experience to begin a new life—and part of that life included marrying my brother! God replaced her sadness and regret with His joy and hope. And He can do the same for you.

Friend, self-control is the trait that makes all of our other captivating characteristics possible. Through self-control we resist the temptation to live by our own rules and instead choose to follow God's ways, which lead us to live with love, to experience joy and peace, and to be patient, kind, gentle, good, and faithful. In Him you'll find all you need to be magnetic!

Dear Jesus, oh how I need you! My mind tells me to do what I want and what feels good now. Yet I also know what I sow, I will reap. Empower me through the Holy Spirit to sow obedience in practicing self-control so I can gain Your best for my life! Amen.

Maintaining the Magnetism

Fruit for a Lifetime

I sure have enjoyed this time with you! I think of you and pray for you often. I hope you have gained a whole new perspective on what godly guys are looking for, but most of all, a deeper understanding of the traits Jesus wants to shine through you.

There is only one way to keep the magnetic glow going: spending time in God's Word and talking with Him every day. The girl who wants a swim-team scholarship swims every day. The one who dreams of a singing career sings every day. The girl who wants to become magnetic spends time with the Magnetic One every day. Becoming the girl He wants will be the natural outcome.

As we wrap up our time together, I want to encourage you: God is doing a great work in your life. Some days, you might feel like just the opposite, as if nothing is going the right direction and, in fact, your life stinks! But God says in Philippians 2:13, "For it is God who works in you to will and to act according to his good purpose." He started a good work in you, and He will keep on working. For His good and yours.

Your part is to keep partnering with Him, surrendering to His ways over your own, being patient as He unfolds His plans.

WAITING ON GOD

Getting to God's best rarely happens quickly. One of the hardest areas to wait for His best is in your love life. As I interviewed people for *Magnetic*, though, I saw a pattern: so many couples waited a long time to find each other.

This was certainly true for Adam and Lindsay. Adam told me, "I waited a long time to find Lindsay, but I knew she was out there. I believe God gave me the desire to be with someone and He wouldn't have given me that desire if there weren't someone for me. I know that waiting and being patient isn't what anyone wants to hear, but it's true! I can't tell you enough how in Lindsay I got more than I ever wanted, thought I wanted, or I could have imagined. Before Lindsay came, though, I had to become okay with being single and I had to trust all along that God was taking care of it."

Lindsay also said the waiting was not easy. "I say I waited thirty years for Adam because we didn't meet until I was turning thirty," she explained. "Waiting that long was hard! My twin sister got married when we were twenty-four. I couldn't understand why God allowed her to have a husband when I didn't have one."

Does that question sound familiar? *Why not me, God?*

"I prayed and prayed. I cried and cried," Lindsay said. "My heart ached; I was so lonely. I don't know really how you get through the waiting time without any of these feelings, but I do know that all of those years, days, and hours brought Adam and me to the appointed time and place God had planned. I really think our relationship would not have the depth or authenticity it has if we hadn't had the wait. God knows what you need and when you need it."

During the time when she wanted a guy in her life but didn't have one, Lindsay said she often looked to the encouragement she found in Genesis 16:13: "You are the God who sees me."

Let's check out the story behind this verse. The character in our story is a young woman named Hagar, a slave to a woman named Sarai. (You might have heard of Sarai before. Later on in the book of Genesis she is renamed Sarah.) Though she desperately wanted to have a child, Sarai was way past that stage of her life. I'm talking old; her husband was eighty-six! But she came up with a plan, knowing that according to the customs of the day, if her servant girl got pregnant, Sarai could claim the child as her own.

So Sarai approached her husband, Abram (later called Abraham) with the idea.

Sarai: "How about if you sleep with my slave, get her pregnant, and I can get a child that way."

Abram: "What have I got to lose?"

Soon Hagar was pregnant with Abram's child. That's when the real trouble started! Hagar started to look down on her mistress, since Sarai couldn't have a baby. Sarai got angry about her slave's attitude, blamed Abram, and informed him he needed to deal with the situation. (How's that for girl drama?)

Abram, after getting chewed out, passed the responsibility for dealing with Hagar right back to his wife. Sarai let her anger loose, treating Hagar so roughly she ran away into the desert.

Out in the middle of nowhere, Hagar encountered the angel of the Lord by a fountain. He instructed her to return to Sarai and Abram, but he also gave her this promise: "I will so increase your descendants that they will be too numerous to count" (Genesis 16:10). If her descendants will be too many to count, she and her son were not going to die! Hagar responded, "You are the God who sees me.... I have now seen the One who sees me" (verse 13). The promise reassured Hagar that God saw all the pain she was going through and He would be with her.

This is the same promise Lindsay relied on. Though she often felt alone, she found hope knowing God saw her. He would take care of her.

Nothing Less Than God's Best

Lindsay shared powerful advice for any girl who's still waiting for the right guy: "Try learning from every lonely moment and broken heart. Ask God to teach or reveal something each second you feel a spark of jealousy or loneliness creeping in. Don't waste the wait. If He has you waiting, get all that you can out of it. You might as well. You can't skip it."

This advice to make the most of waiting was shared by many people I spoke with. Samantha told me, "I got married a lot later than I had thought or hoped I would. Honestly, I longed to be married in my early twenties and have a whole bunch of kids by now. But that isn't how it worked out. Waiting for Josh was difficult but worth it. There were many times I could have compromised and married a guy who didn't really follow God. Now that I'm married, I see how much harder life would have been if I'd done that."

According to Samantha, waiting isn't something to just be endured. It's an opportunity to prepare yourself for whatever God has for your future. "Here's my takeaway from waiting," she said. "Invest your time and energy into serving others. Do things you love. Save your money and get wise counsel on how to spend it. Study Scripture and grow your relationship with Jesus. Really get to know Him and fall in love with Him. Spend time with your family and friends. Have fun, enjoy life, resting in the truth God is for you and has good plans for you. I had to settle in my heart if I never got married, I would be okay. Yes, I had to let go of some dreams and desires. I learned how to trust that God loved me and experienced His peace either way. Pray according to His Word and His will, and don't settle."

Samantha's advice, along with the comments of so many others who waited a long time, leads me to believe that often we need time to develop the character required for a God-honoring relationship. Our level of spiritual maturity has a lot to do with the type of person we are attracted to as well as attract. We need time to become magnetic.

If you were a godly guy, would you date you? Why or why not?

. . . .
. . . .
. . . .
. . . .
. . . .
. . . .

Part of the reason for our waiting is because God will not allow us to find satisfaction in something or someone other than Himself. He's a jealous God. That sounds like an oxymoron, our perfect God being jealous. But He is jealous for you because He knows that you will only be truly joy filled when you find all you are looking for in Him.

In Hosea 2:7 God is speaking of His people: "She will chase after her lovers but not catch them; she will look for them but not find them. Then she will say, 'I will go back to my husband as at first, for then I was better off than now.'" God knows that we are human and are tempted to try to find the love and life we are looking for in places other than Him. He says that we will chase but not find what we are looking for. When we are worn out from all this running, we will turn to Him.

If you can't figure out why God hasn't given you what you have asked for, ask Him, *Is it the wrong time in my life? Do I want a guy I can touch more than I want the God who can touch my heart?*

Because He made us, God gets us. He speaks to us, "Therefore I am now going to allure her; I will lead her...and speak tenderly to her" (Hosea 2:14). God is so kind to us in our imperfection. He comes after us, tenderly leading us back to Him. He is with you, meeting you where you need Him most. "I led them with cords of human kindness, with ties of love; I lifted the yoke from their neck and bent down to feed them" (Hosea 11:4). I love this verse! He is kind, loves us so much, and bends down to meet us where we are in order to take care of us!

When you respond to His love by seeking Him with all of your heart, you will find the joy and love you were designed to experience. You will find His fruit of the Spirit in your life, and it will be beautiful! "Sow for yourselves righteousness, reap the fruit of unfailing love, and break up your unplowed ground; for it is time to seek the LORD, until he comes and showers righteousness on you" (Hosea 10:12).

DAILY BECOMING MAGNETIC

Now you know the truth about becoming the girl He wants. The question is, will you live it out? Will you seek to let His life shine through you, or will you chase after your own desires? The answer won't be determined by a once-for-all decision but by your daily, moment-by-moment choices.

I'll confess sometimes I've found it difficult to give up what I want, even when I knew it wasn't God's best for me.

After high school, I attended a Christian training school a thousand miles from home. With no companions, no car, and no connections, it was a lonely time in my life. I've since learned that these tough spots are often the times when temptation targets us.

I had just made up my mind to not date for a time and to focus 100 percent of my attention on filling my heart with Jesus's love—and that's when my crush of over seven years contacted me. (You know, I don't even know how he got my number!) This wasn't a bad thing; he was a great guy. It was an opportunity for me to make a decision. What was the wise thing?

Sometimes I think "What is the wise thing?" is even harder to answer than "Is this a bad thing?" Good and bad are usually obvious; wise and unwise can be a bit harder. I made one of the hardest decisions of my life. After a few days, with heart pounding and eyes crying, I let my crush know I wasn't in a place for a relationship. This decision was wise—and hard.

That one decision, next to my decision to make Christ my Savior, was one of the best decisions I ever made. I learned I can trust God with even the most important heart desires. I learned the Holy Spirit empowers me with all I need to get God's best each and every time in my life.

And I did get His best! Later, after I had learned that only Jesus could completely fill me, my crush and I did get together…and Greg and I eventually got married!

I am not saying that if you obey Jesus, He will give you what you want every time. Sometimes what we think is best for us really isn't. What I am saying is that our obedience opens doors in our lives for His best, which is exactly what He wants to give us! Here's how He says it: "Delight yourself in the LORD and he will give you the desires of your heart" (Psalm 37:4).

Friend, I hope this study is just the beginning of your digging into

God's Word for yourself, because He has so much more to teach you about becoming magnetic. Open His love letter, the Bible, each and every day, and keep on becoming magnetic!

> *Jesus, I have learned so much about You and about godly guys too! I want to be magnetic, producing the fruit of the Spirit, my whole lifetime. Please bring back to my memory the things I have learned and produce lifelong change in me. Amen.*

Captivating Quiz Results

Love ____ points

Kindness ____ points

Gentleness ____ points

Joy ____ points

Goodness ____ points

Peace ____ points

Faithfulness ____ points

Patience ____ points

Self-Control ____ points

On which quiz did you score the highest? _____

This is the area in which you are the strongest. This could be an indication of one of your spiritual gifts. Focus on sharing this trait with others around you!

On which did you score the lowest? _____

This is the area in which you are the weakest. Make this trait a point of daily prayer, and look for the Holy Spirit to fill you with His strength to grow more magnetic!

The *Magnetic* Manifesto

To become the girl He wants I will...

Love others as I love myself; this will be obvious by the way I treat others. (Matthew 22:39)

Look for *joy* in the present rather than focusing on what seems to be missing. (Isaiah 35:10)

Go after *peace,* asking for prayers to pray, not words to say. (Psalm 34:14)

Be *patient.* I'll wait; not manipulate. (Proverbs 14:29)

In *kindness,* put others' needs and desires above my own. (Jeremiah 9:23–24)

Choose *goodness* to stand strong, not just go along. (Ephesians 5:3–4)

Fight to be *faithful,* not quick to let go of something great to snatch something better. (Proverbs 3:3)

Lean into God's *gentleness* to become gentle with myself and others. (Ephesians 4:1–2)

Use *self-control* to not allow feelings-driven thoughts to overrule God's wisdom-living words. (2 Corinthians 12:9–10)

Leader's Guide

Dear Youth Leader, Bible Study Leader, Small Group Leader, Mom,

Thank you so much for investing in the lives of young women! You are the woman I pray for every day, the one who sees how precious these girls are to God and so they are precious to you too! As a young woman, my life was profoundly impacted by those who took time out of their busy lives to invest in mine. What you are doing will also make an impact on the girls you are investing in. This is how we change the world...one girl at a time. So from the bottom of my heart, thank you!

I wrote this leadership guide to give you the tools you'll need to do the work you have a heart for. For additional help in this adventure, just hop over to my website at www.LynnCowell.com and click on Freebies.

One thing I know: when it comes to investing in girls, you've got to make it fun! While studying God's Word is serious—and I, more than anyone, want them to learn to read and study God's Word—I also know that if it isn't fun, it feels like school. Anything that feels like school is not going to go well!

Here are a few things I love to do with my group to make it fun!

First, we meet in my home. Certainly, you don't have to host the group at your house every time. You might meet at the home of one of the girls, or you could rotate homes. I have just found that girls open up more when you meet in a home versus a restaurant, a coffee shop, or even at church. When they feel cozy, they feel free to talk. So get cozy!

Next, *always* have food—and I do mean always! I don't serve anything fancy. Popcorn, fruit, store-bought cookies. And I don't always provide it. Asking group participants to bring the snack is a great way to get them invested. You can even make the snack together—another great way to teach them!

From here, we start with an icebreaker. My group meets after school, so they need time to debrief, and talking does just that. "If you were a flavor of ice cream, what flavor would you be?" gets conversations rolling (as if girls need help with that!). You can find a list of icebreakers, or conversation starters, on my website under Freebies. I printed these conversation starters out, cut them up, and put them in a vase. Each week one of the girls in the group takes turns choosing one.

Here's another important goal: laughter. Laughter is good for you, and it's good for them! I used to be wound so tight about getting through all the material each week. What I was really doing was stifling conversation, cutting them off when we should have been digging in. Don't worry if you don't get to all the questions. If the girls want to continue working through the same chapter next time you get together, great! If you just want to move on, that's okay too. The Holy Spirit knows what He's doing; let Him do it!

I love to give a prize if they answer the questions in their books before they arrive. This motivates them to read their chapter and take the time to answer the questions ahead of time. Sometimes I'll see who answered the questions, put their names in a bowl, and draw a winner. Other times, I give something small to each person. Every little motivator helps! If I find most of the girls have not already read the chapter and answered the questions, we'll choose to read much of the material out loud together, because it's almost impossible to have a quality discussion on a topic no one has read. This is not my favorite way, as it can develop into a pattern. A little grace goes a long way, though! These girls have so much on their plate; they don't need any additional pressure. Instead, they need a ton of hugs, a gob of unconditional love, and a woman they can tell anything to. Thank you in advance for being that woman!

When going through *Magnetic,* help the girls memorize Galatians 5:22–23. Again, you might offer rewards to increase their motivation.

Setting aside chapter 11 (the conclusion), *Magnetic* has ten chapters that include questions, quizzes, and biblical principles to help guide a girl's understanding of what it looks like to shine with the fruit of the Spirit. So you might find it best to plan on covering a chapter a week for ten weeks, then reserve one additional week to wrap up the discussion and celebrate all you've learned together. In the pages that follow, you'll find specific guidelines and discussion questions for each week, but the basic pattern for each group meeting would look like this:

- Prayer.
- Icebreaker.
- Go over sticky statements (see below).
- Discuss their answers to the in-chapter questions and anything else they highlighted.
- Use the provided leader's guide questions.
- Share prayer requests, then pray together.
- Remind the girls to read, highlight, and answer questions in the next chapter before you meet again.

Let's get started!

CHAPTER 1
The Power to Become Magnetic

At your first meeting together, have the girls share their name, school, and something they like about themselves. Encourage the girls to invite other girls to join the group, especially at the beginning.

Read chapter 1 out loud. This is really important as it provides a road map for the study and sets the expectation that we are all going to work with the Holy Spirit to allow Him to change us! Discuss memorizing Galatians 5:22–23 together and practice for a bit. Have a question-and-answer time, giving them an opportunity to clarify what to expect in the weeks come.

I also like to emphasize some key phrases, what I call sticky statements, in each chapter. I refer to them as sticky because these short bits of truth are easy to memorize. When they come to our mind in the middle of a situation, they can help us change our behavior. You'll recognize these within each chapter because they're often set apart from text in a curlicue frame. Some chapters have just one or two; some several. The one for chapter 1 is:

- *Nothing on this planet should hold you back from your purpose, especially not some guy!*

In my group, I like to point out each sticky statement, encouraging the girls to think about that point throughout the coming week. Texting group members this phrase midweek can also bring it to their thoughts.

Finish your time together by sharing prayer requests. My group keeps a notebook in which we write down our prayer requests so we can watch to see how God answers them! Encourage each girl to read chapter 2, on love, before the next meeting. Tell them to highlight the stuff they like and any important ideas as they read. This can really help discussion the following week. Also encourage them to put a question mark next to anything they didn't get or have more questions about.

Keep in mind, this first week is where you'll set the standard for how the rest of the weeks will go. Really emphasize that this group is *their* group, and this study is *their* study. If everyone reads during the week, it means we all grow and learn more when we get together!

CHAPTER 2
It's (Not) All About Me: Love

After your icebreaker, begin by going over Galatians 5:22–23. Make it the goal of the group to memorize this passage before the end of the book. Challenge them to break it down into pieces to make memorizing easier. Then move on to the discussion questions.

Throughout your discussion today, look for opportunities to emphasize some of this chapter's sticky statements. Here are two sticky statements for this week's lesson:

- *When I make love all about* me, *I ruin the chance to focus on* we.
- *Another's failure never makes us look better.*

Discussion Questions

1. Can you think of a time when you, like Kalley, didn't want to do something but love said you would?

2. Since we use *love* to describe how we feel about everything from fashion to family, what is our definition for *love* when it comes to how we treat others?

3. Have a girl in the group explain the love cycle: God loves us, we love God, we love others, together we love God. (When I taught my group, I drew it out on a piece of paper in a circle.)

4. Why would a guy find unselfish love attractive?

5. Discuss the different types of love discussed in chapter 2. Ask the girls to give examples of these types of loves in their lives and to explain how they differ.

6. Why are girls sometimes happy over someone else's trouble? Discuss insecurity's impact on our outlook.

After wrapping up with prayer, remind the girls to read chapter 3 before next week, making sure to highlight, underline, and put question marks in the margins.

CHAPTER 3
Adjusting Our Expectations: Joy

After opening with prayer and an icebreaker, begin by going over Galatians 5:22–23 again. Maybe one or two of your girls already have verse 22 memorized. They can cheer on the others!

As you go through the questions the girls have written in the margins of their books and cover this week's discussion questions, look for ways to include this week's sticky statements:

- *Unwavering joy can't come from an unpredictable boy.*
- *Boyfriend-based identity crumbles with a breakup.*
- *Don't hang your joy on waiting for "the one." Seek Him— not him!*

Discussion Questions

1. Think back to your childhood. What is your first joyful memory?
2. In Psalm 31:7, where did David say he got his joy from?
3. In Nehemiah 8:10, what did Nehemiah say was the source of his strength?
4. Do you have a joy robber in the form of a person or place working overtime to drain your heart?
5. Based on the story from John 5, what is your "mat"—the thing you need to get rid of or the habit you need to kick in order to get Jesus's joy in your life?

6. What three commands did David give us in 1 Chronicles 16:7–8 to help us kick the habit?

Wrap up with prayer.

CHAPTER 4
Drop the Drama: Peace

Since you'll be talking today about girl drama, for your icebreaker start by playing the old-fashioned game of Telephone, where one person whispers a word or phrase to the girl next to her, then each in turn whispers it to the next person. The last person repeats out loud what she heard—and you get to hear how it changed along the way! This will set the stage to talk about the power of gossip.

Hopefully by this point, your group is beginning to remember key phrases from Galatians 5:22–23. This week's sticky statements include:

- *Ask Jesus for prayers to pray, not words to say.*
- *Peace is the power choice of the magnetic girl.*
- *The God who keeps the world spinning can take care of my spinning!*

Discussion Questions

1. When you were a child, was your house peaceful? Why or why not?
2. Read Proverbs 17:9. Why would love cover over an offense? Have you ever covered over an offense? When?
3. As a group, rewrite Proverbs 17:19, putting it in everyday words.
4. Which is easier for you: talk it out or let it go? Why? Have

you ever tried talking it out with God before you talk it out with your friend? Did it help?

5. Read Philippians 4:6–9 together. What do these verses say we should we be anxious for? How do we get away from anxiety? Review the steps for CPR given in the chapter.

6. Do people, places, or problems steal your peace? How?

Before you close in prayer, wrap up by reading Matthew 6:25–32 out loud.

CHAPTER 5
Wait Training 101: Patience

With prayer as your opener, draw out an icebreaker question to start your group time. There are probably a few in your group who can repeat Galatians 5:22–23 completely. Consider rewarding them for their effort. This week's sticky statements to weave throughout the conversation include:

- *Wait. Let God orchestrate.*
- *Knowing we're chosen by Jesus, we can wait to be chosen by another.*
- *Wait. Don't manipulate.*
- *Impatience outside reveals agitation inside.*

Discussion Questions

1. How many times does David say "do not fret" just in Psalm 37:1–9? Why do you think he says it so many times?

2. In Psalm 37, what connection do you find between verse 5 and verse 7?

3. Is it okay to make the first move with a guy? Why or why not?

4. Where do you draw the line between being friendly and being aggressive?

5. Why can it be so hard to believe God is on your side, working for your best and His?

6. Share a story of when impatience gave you a "black eye," a time when your impatience turned embarrassing.

7. What does "Wait; let God orchestrate" mean?

Chapter 6
No Need to Be Mean About It: Kindness

Ask one of your girls to open with prayer today and another to lead the icebreaker. Giving them roles to play encourages members to view this as *their* group, not yours.

You're over halfway done! I hope by now your group is really engaging in the concept of taking their focus off the guys and putting it on God. Keep reviewing Galatians 5:22–23. My sticky statement for this week is…

- *The kind girl is the kind he wants.*

Also cover:

- *Those who respect you the most should be the ones who know you the best. —Andy Stanley*

- *If you're not out of your comfort zone, you aren't doing something right. —Steven Furtick*

Discussion Questions

1. Look up Psalm 41:1–3, then list the joys and blessings of those who are kind to the poor.

2. Psalm 41:1–3 says to have "regard for the weak." What does this look like in your life?

3. Twenty years from now, if you were to become a wife and mom, how would you want your husband and children to describe you? List some adjectives.

4. How has Jesus been kind to you?

5. Read Galatians 6:7–8. How can you sow kindness? What would it look like to reap kindness?

6. Based on this chapter, is there an action God is asking you to take regarding kindness?

7. Read Galatians 2:20. What would it mean if we were to say we are "better off dead"?

Ask the girls to text each other a prayer, a verse, or the sticky statement as a way to encourage each other during the week.

CHAPTER 7
Beauty in a Pure Heart: Goodness

To shake things up a bit, start out group today with a bag of M&M'S. Randomly give one to every person. Ask each girl to share what this color reminds her of: something in nature, a favorite sweatshirt, and so on.

By now, everyone probably knows Galatians 5:22–23. Simply review. This week's sticky statements include:

- *Good girls don't just go along—they stand strong.*
- *What we pour in pours out!*

Discussion Questions

In chapter 7, I ask the question, "Have you asked Jesus to forgive you for your sins and give you His new life? Write out what that experience has looked like." Today, reread the explanation of salvation on page 114 and be sure every girl understands salvation. Share with the girls your story of how Jesus became your personal Savior. Be sensitive to the Holy Spirit concerning the details, sharing only age-appropriate information.

1. Ask if anyone in the group would be willing to share her story of starting her relationship with Jesus. This will take a long time, maybe even the whole group time. If so, you can just pick up next week at chapter 7 again.

2. Describe a time in your life when you were caught in a situation that was not good for you but you didn't really see it.

3. What types of dopey decisions do you see happening around you that affect people for a long time?

4. Second Peter 1:5–9 speaks of a progression of growth for us as Christ followers. In the last verse, Peter says, "But if anyone does not have them [the traits listed in the prior verses], he is nearsighted and blind, and has forgotten that he has been cleansed from his past sins." Why would the lack of these traits in a Christian's life be an indication she has forgotten Christ's forgiveness?

5. What reward comes to those who plan good? (Read Proverbs 14:22.)

6. Read this statement: *Good girls don't just go along—they stand strong.* What does it mean, and why is it important?

Invite the girls to share their prayer requests. Then go around the circle to pray, having each girl pray for the girl on her right.

CHAPTER 8
No Matter What: Faithfulness

For this week's icebreaker, bring a ball of yarn, jute, or something similar. Ask each girl to cut a portion for a string. Then have each girl put her thumb and index finger from the same hand at the top of the string. Have her put her thumb and index finger of the other hand under it, inching down the whole length of the string. While she is doing this, have her share things about herself, such as "I like Reese's peanut butter cups" and other fun facts the group may not know.

It may feel monotonous to continue reciting Galatians 5:22–23. Don't give up. These verses will serve all the girls for the rest of their lives!

Our sticky statements for this chapter include:

- *Choosing the easy path instead of the right one could cost us everything.*
- *Faithfulness is a deal maker or deal breaker.*
- *Don't be too quick to let go of something good in order to snatch at something seemingly better.*
- *Flirting can cause relationship failure; faithfulness proves his heart is safe with you.*
- *If you don't have trust, your relationship has nothing to stand on.*

Discussion Questions

1. In your future, what relationships do you see requiring faithfulness?

2. Read Psalm 15 together, preferably in a modern translation. As you read the description of a person who is close to God, what are some adjectives you would use to describe this individual?

3. When have you struggled with jealousy in seeing others getting away with something they shouldn't have? Are you struggling now? Read Proverbs 23:17–19 for reinforcement.

4. Read the words from the hymn "Come, Thou Fount of Every Blessing." (You can find them on the Internet.) Why are our hearts "prone to wander"?

5. When you are dating a guy, do you think it is okay to flirt with other guys, call them, hang out with them? Why or why not? Discuss the sticky statement *Flirting can cause relationship failure; faithfulness proves his heart is safe with you.*

6. Have you experienced the flirting high Lynn wrote about?

7. Why is faithfulness so important in a relationship?

Invite one girl in the group to wrap up in prayer.

CHAPTER 9
A Tender Touch: Gentleness

When going over Galatians 5:22–23, purposefully change the order of the traits and see who notices. Our sticky statements include:

- *When I lean in to the gentle side of God, I become gentle with myself and others.*
- *Keep conflict classy! Carefully choose your words.*

Discussion Questions

1. Have you ever had someone describe you using words that might be considered the opposite of gentleness? What were those words?

2. Read Hosea 11:4 out loud. Does this verse evoke any emotion? How does it fit with or go against the way you have thought of God in the past?

3. In what situations do you struggle to be gentle?

4. Do you feel like you are carrying a weight or a burden? What overwhelms your heart?

5. Read Matthew 11:28–30: "Come to me, all you who are weary and burdened, and I will give you rest. Take my yoke

upon you and learn from me, for I am gentle and humble in heart, and you will find rest for your souls. For my yoke is easy and my burden is light." How does knowing God wants to carry your burdens help you in becoming a gentler person?

6. Is there an area in your life where you are harsh on yourself and hard on others? Talk about the statement *Hard on myself = Hard on others.*

7. Read this statement: *When I lean into the gentle side of God, I become gentle with myself.* Why is this true?

CHAPTER 10
Keeping Your Cool: Self-Control

Write out Galatians 5:22–23 on a poster board and then cut out the words. Have your group put the words together to create the passage. Our last sticky statements include:

- *Use your words to draw others to you, not drive them from you.*
- *Self-control says no to situations where your standards can be seduced.*
- *Trouble comes when feelings-driven thoughts overrule God's wisdom-living words.*
- *The choices I make today determine the course of my tomorrows.*
- *If we are not intentional about where we are going, we are sure to end up where we don't want to be.*

Discussion Questions

1. See if the girls are willing to share where they struggle with self-control the most. If you will go first, it will help them to be more vulnerable.

2. With their struggle, help them fill in the blank or share
   if they already did: "I want _____ so that
   _____."

3. Why does God tell us, "For wherever there is jealousy
   and selfish ambition, there you will find disorder and evil
   of every kind" (James 3:16, NLT)? How does this fit the
   statement *God's wisdom-living words overrule feelings-driven
   actions.*

4. Why does Proverbs 29:25 say, "Fearing people is a dangerous
   trap" (NLT)?

5. "But seek first his kingdom and his righteousness, and all
   these things will be given to you as well" (Matthew 6:33).
   What things will God add to our lives if we seek Him
   first?

6. Lynn wrote, "Contentment settles his fears. No need to
   worry he won't be able to give her the stuff she wants
   because she already has all her needs met through God!"
   What would a guy fear?

CHAPTER 11
Maintaining the Magnetism

Use this week to celebrate completing the study. Maybe make a meal together, go out to dinner, or have a themed potluck. Afterward, ask the
girls to share how they have seen *Magnetic* change their lives. Continue
the discussion with a few of these questions:

1. What has God taught you?

2. How has your thinking about guys changed?

3. How has your thinking about yourself changed?

4. What were your favorite chapters?

Encourage the girls to keep *Magnetic* as a resource to go back to as they continue their journey with God and navigating relationships.

Thank you so much for all you have done, friend, to pour God's truth into these precious girls. Well done! You did it!

Dear Mom

From one mom of teen girls to another, I want to tell you I am proud of you! By picking up *Magnetic: Becoming the Girl He Wants,* you're showing a glimpse of your heart and how you want God's best for your girl.

So I wanted to share my heart with you—my heart for your daughter and for my own girls. These teen years can be nothing short of turbulent. I don't have to tell you that; you've lived them and are, to some degree, living them again with your girl. It is now, in this season when life-altering decisions are made, that our girls need us more than ever. Even if their words and body language say differently, they want to know we care for them and about them. And they want our help. Maybe not in a way that tells them what to do, but in a way that helps them find what they need to find: true love and security in the unconditional, perfect love of a Savior, along with the tools to sort out and discern the other loves that touch our girls' hearts.

My goal is not so much to mentor your girl but to come alongside you as you intentionally invest in her life. That's why I included a leader's guide, a resource for you to use if you read *Magnetic* together. You'll find other free resources to empower you on this journey at my website—www.LynnCowell.com—as well as the opportunity to connect with other moms raising wiser daughters too. One thing I hear often from moms through social media and my conferences is "Thank you for saying the same things I am saying." As moms, we need one another to be voices speaking truth through all the noise.

So thank you for empowering your daughter with the truth of God's Word and with the truth of what it means to be a woman making wise choices and honoring God. Thank you for choosing to pour true love into her tender heart every day.

His,

Lynn

Notes

1. Melinda Beck, "Thank You. No, Thank You," *Wall Street Journal,* November 23, 2010, http://online.wsj.com/news/articles/SB100014 24052748704243904575630541486290052.

2. Lynn Cowell, *His Revolutionary Love* (Cincinnati, OH: Standard, 2011), 85.

3. Alexandra C, "My Spinal Fusion Surgery Story," September 20, 2012, www.youtube.com/watch?v=cCj7Ps7V4rY.

4. Mark Batterson, *In a Pit with a Lion on a Snowy Day* (Colorado Springs: Multnomah, 2006), 15.

5. David Simons, "Think Like a Marketer, Act Like a Consumer," May 8, 2012, *Soshable* (blog), http://soshable.com/think-like-a -marketer-operate-as-a-consumer.

6. Jeremy Dean, "Practicing Gratitude Can Increase Happiness by 25%," *PsyBlog,* September 10, 2007, www.spring.org.uk/2007/09 /practicing-gratitude-can-increase.php.

7. Louann Brizendine, MD, *The Female Brain* (New York: Morgan Road, 2006), 14.

8. Shaunti Feldhahn, *For Women Only,* rev. ed. (Colorado Springs: Multnomah, 2013), 16–17.

9. Lysa TerKeurst, Twitter post, July 11, 2013, 5:20 p.m., https:// twitter.com/LysaTerKeurst/status/355481863223119872.

About Proverbs 31 Ministries

If you were inspired by *Magnetic: Becoming the Girl He Wants* and desire to deepen your own personal relationship with Jesus Christ, I encourage you to connect with Proverbs 31 Ministries.

Proverbs 31 Ministries exists to be a trusted friend who will take you by the hand and walk by your side, leading you one step closer to the heart of God through

- free online daily devotions
- COMPEL writing community
- daily radio program
- books and resources
- online Bible studies

To learn more about Proverbs 31 Ministries or to inquire about having Lynn Cowell speak at your event, call 877-731-4663 or visit www .Proverbs31.org.

Proverbs 31 Ministries
630 Team Road, Suite 100
Matthews, NC 28105
www.Proverbs31.org